Gayle Soucek

Parakeets

Everything About Selection, Care,
Nutrition, Behavior, and Training

BARRON'S

CONTENTS

Introduction to Parakeets ... 5

Budgies in the Wild ... 7

The Parakeet Personality ... 8

Is a Parakeet Right For Me? ... 8

Will My Parakeet Talk? ... 9

Parakeets and Children ... 10

Parakeets and the Elderly ... 10

Buying a Companion Parakeet ... 13

Does Sex Matter? ... 13

One Bird or Two? ... 14

Colors and Mutations ... 16

Where to Find Parakeets ... 17

Finding an Avian Veterinarian ... 20

HOW-TO: Choosing a Healthy Parakeet ... 22

Bringing Home Your Pet ... 25

Choosing a Cage ... 25

Cage Location ... 28

Air Quality ... 29

The Right Light ... 30

Temperature ... 32

Quarantine ... 33

Diet for a Healthy Parakeet ... 35

The Basics ... 37

Dry Food Storage ... 39

Insects and Rodents ... 39

Fresh Foods ... 40

Cooked Diets and People Food ... 43

Treats ... 43

Supplements ... 44

The Daily Routine ... 47

Daily Tasks ... 47

Weekly Tasks ... 49

As Needed Chores ... 49

Bathing and Grooming ... 49

Playtime ... 53

Birdie Bedtime ... 55

Understanding Your Parakeet ... 59

The Life of a Prey Animal ... 59

The Flock Mentality ... 60

The Pet Parakeet ... 61

Bonding and Imprinting ... 62

Taming and Training Your Parakeet ... 65

Speech Training ... 66

Trick Training ... 68

HOW-TO: Understanding Parakeet Body Language ... 70

Common Illnesses and Health Care ... 73

At the Veterinarian's Office ... 74

Home Care ... 77

Common Diseases ... 77

Malnutrition ... 78

Bacterial Infections ... 79

Chlamydiosis ... 79

Avian Polyomavirus (APV) ... 80

Psittacine Beak and Feather Disease (PBFD) ... 81

Scaly Face ... 81

Parakeet First Aid ... 83

Household Hazards ... 83

First Aid ... 85

What to Do if Your Parakeet Gets Lost ... 90

Information ... 92

Index ... 94

INTRODUCTION TO PARAKEETS

Parakeets are small, inquisitive birds that need a lot of love and attention to thrive.

In the arid scrub land of Australia's outback, survival is often determined by adaptability. The climate is harsh and capricious, and water is usually in short supply. Some years pass with no measurable rainfall at all in the central deserts. In other years, the tails of northern monsoons dip down toward the interior and flash floods roar across the red sandy soil, leaving behind brackish muddy watering holes for the birds and animals that inhabit the area.

Perhaps the most adaptable residents are the birds; Australia boasts nearly 800 different species, including fifty-six from the parrot family. These range from the extraordinarily rare and unusual night parrot (*Pezoporus occidentalis*) to the common and easily recognizable budgerigar (*Melopsittacus undulates*). To most Americans, the Australian budgerigar, or "budgie," is simply known as a parakeet, but in reality the name "parakeet" is a rather

loose descriptor that is applied to any number of slim-bodied, long-tailed parrots found throughout Australia, Asia, Africa, and South America. In fact, roughly twenty-one of Australia's parrots are commonly classed as parakeets, or simply "keets" for short. And the term can be applied inconsistently, depending on the locale. For example, *Neopsephotus bourkii* is known in Australia as Bourke's parrot, but in the United States the bird is called a Bourke's parakeet.

Confused yet? To put it simply, that familiar little chirpy green or blue pet bird that is for sale in almost every pet shop in the country can be correctly identified as a budgerigar, budgie, parakeet, or small parrot. This illustrates why scientists and serious aviculturists often use the Latin names of the species—not to impress people with their grasp of Latin, but to avoid the confusion that can occur when

dealing with species that are known by various common names throughout the world. In this book, we will focus solely on the Australian budgerigar, but in the interest of avoiding repetition, I will use the terms budgie, parakeet, and keet interchangeably.

Budgies in the Wild

The origin of the name "budgerigar" is unclear, but most etymologists (people who study word origins) believe that it came from the Australian aboriginal slang *budgery* (good) and *gar* (cockatoo). The word appeared in print in 1847 in Ludwig Leichhardt's *Journal of an Overland Expedition* but was spelled as "betshiregah." The spelling later evolved to "betcherrygah" and finally evolved again to the current "budgerigar," or "budgie." In the 1840s, British ornithologist John Gould gave the feisty little parrots their scientific name, *Melopsittacus undulates.* Genus *Melopsittacus* comes from the Greek and means "melodious parrot." The species name, *undulates,* is from the Latin word for waves, or wave-patterned, and refers to the black and yellow wing patterns of the wild birds.

In fact, all wild budgies are primarily green, with yellow faces and black and yellow barring on their heads, backs, and wings. This is known as the wild or natural color. On rare occasions, a color mutation (usually blue) appears in the wild, but these individuals stand out from the flock and are usually picked off by predators at an early age. In captivity, however, the colors are nearly endless. There are at least thirty-two known color mutations, including pied,

Low Maintenance Myth

I always laugh when I hear people describe birds as low-maintenance pets. I share my life with a variety of parrots and other birds, as well as two large dogs, a cat, and a few reptiles. The birds are by far the highest maintenance. Oh sure, the dogs need love and exercise, along with grooming and regular veterinary visits. So do the birds. The dogs want to be near me whenever I'm home. So do the birds. I have to vacuum up dog and cat hair. I also have to vacuum feathers, tossed food, and bits of chewed woodwork from the parrots. I have to scrub cages, replace perches, cut up fresh foods, replace toys, and generally make myself available for any demands from the feathered household members. The cat mostly sleeps. No, birds are *not* low-maintenance pets. But they are worth every bit of energy they demand.

albino, blue, cinnamon, clearwinged, lutino, mauve, olive, opaline, and spangled, to name a few. These mutations can also combine into hundreds of different individual and sometimes unpredictable colorations.

In addition, there are actually two different "types" of budgies, even though they share the same Latin name. The typical pet budgie is the one most often referred to as the American parakeet, and it is closest in size and shape to its wild ancestors; it stands about 7 inches (18 cm) tall and weighs 1.1–1.4 ounces (30–40 grams). Another type, the English budgie (also known as the exhibition-type) is much larger—sometimes nearly twice the size—of its American cousins. It is the result of selective breeding and displays an upright posture and large head that is covered with deep, puffy feathers that sometimes almost completely obscure the beak and eyes. Although these are available as pets, they are much more common in bird shows and exhibitions. They are generally considered to have a shorter lifespan than the American keets, but diet and husbandry can greatly impact any bird's longevity. For example, although the average captive lifespan of an American parakeet is about five years, there are documented cases of keets living well into their twenties.

The Parakeet Personality

Parakeets are gregarious and inquisitive little birds that sometimes forget they're little birds! They pack a lot of personality and charm into their bodies and have an expansive nature that puts them on par with larger birds in terms of pet appeal. It's not easy to describe a typical parakeet; their intelligence gives them a lot of individuality. In almost all cases, however, they will thrive in a household that offers them a lot of love and security. If you are considering adding a keet to your life, you must realize that they are not simply colorful, animated decorations; they are sentient and sensitive creatures that need lots of attention and affection.

Is a Parakeet Right for Me?

Before you make the decision to bring home a pet parakeet, ask yourself the following questions:

✔ Am I willing to spend the money necessary to provide a healthy diet, stimulating toys, and necessary veterinary care for the bird?

✔ Do I have enough room for a spacious cage and a safe play area for an active keet?

✔ Do I have time to devote on a daily basis to play with my bird and satisfy its emotional need for companionship?

✔ Do I have other pets that might pose a threat to a caged bird? Am I willing and able to control those pets safely?

✔ Do I live with family members or housemates that might object to a new pet?

✔ Do I have small children that need to be taught proper handling methods for a relatively defenseless small bird? Will the children obey, or inadvertently torture the bird?

✔ Am I willing to clean and feed the parakeet on a daily basis?

✔ If I travel, is there someone who can be trusted to bird-sit?

✔ Do I (or a household member) have allergies or asthma that might be exacerbated by the feather dander and dust produced by a healthy parakeet?

✔ Do I truly want to share my life with this creature, or am I acting on a whim or buying a talking toy for my children?

✔ Do I understand that this pet has a potential lifespan of twenty years or more, and am I willing to accept such a long commitment?

If you still want a parakeet after considering the above questions, congratulations! You have made the decision intelligently and will have the knowledge to provide a happy, healthy home for your pet.

Will My Parakeet Talk?

The answer to this question is a qualified "maybe." All parakeets have the vocal mechanism to mimic human speech, and they certainly have the intelligence. The real question is whether they have the desire. Some birds love to talk and will quiver in delight as they listen closely to every word you utter. These overachievers practice speech at every opportunity and can develop huge vocabularies. As a matter of fact, it is a budgie named Puck that holds the *Guinness Book of World Records* title as the bird with the largest vocabulary, clocking in with a staggering 1,728 words. Most talking birds fall far from that target and might just learn a few dozen words. And some birds never speak a single word. Apparently, they just don't have anything to say.

If your primary goal is to purchase a parakeet that is guaranteed to talk, however, you are buying the bird for all the wrong reasons. You should acquire a pet based on its ability to share love and provide companionship; talking is just a side benefit from a happy bird. Your pet will be most likely to mimic you if you speak to it with an enthusiastic and slightly higher-pitched voice. Low monotones are boring to birds. Use repetition, but only as long as your keet is interested and engaged. If possible,

use appropriate words, such as "treat" while offering a treat, "good night" while covering the cage, and so on. Parakeets can learn meaningful speech with consistent training. In fact, after hearing non-stop choruses of "pretty bird" and spending hours listening to off-key renditions of the *Andy Griffith Show* theme song, you might find yourself wishing that the darn bird would just shut up. Enjoy your parakeet's silly antics and affectionate nature, and always think twice before you play old sitcom themes within earshot of the bird.

Parakeets and Children

Keets can be wonderful companions for children as long as parents are willing to set some guidelines and supervise the care and play. It's difficult to set a "minimum age" for interaction, because it depends greatly on the child's level of maturity and empathy; some 5-year-olds are perfect caretakers, while other kids aren't responsible enough until they are much older. (And, unfortunately, even some adults never develop the instincts to properly care for a helpless and dependent creature.)

In any case, when buying a parakeet as a child's pet, always be aware that the primary responsibility falls upon the adult. It's wonderful to use a pet to teach a child responsibility, but please don't let the bird suffer if the child forgets to perform an aspect of care. If you allow the keet to go hungry or thirsty to drive home a point, you're being cruel to the child and the pet. And please don't dump the parakeet if your child's interest in the bird wanes. You will only be teaching that it's acceptable to shirk love and responsibility on a whim, and once again, it will be the innocent animal that suffers the most.

To facilitate the relationship, spend some time teaching the child budgie-appropriate games. I often see kids sticking their fingers into a bird's cage, and then jerking back when the bird reaches out with its beak. To the youngster, this is a thrilling game of "catch me if you can." To the bird, this is a frustrating and confusing violation of its territory and its trust, and can lead to aggressive biting. Of course the kids mean no harm, but they've never been taught the difference between playing and teasing from a parakeet's viewpoint. Chapter 5 has some ideas on playtime to get you started, and as your understanding of the bird develops, you'll soon know what your pet thinks is fun, and what it dislikes.

I also suggest that parents spend some time discussing what it means when a pet bird acts fearful or aggressive. Sensitive children might react with hurt or anger because they feel rejected by the pet. If you explain that the bird is just trying to communicate without words, and it is still their friend, you can help heal the relationship when it goes through some inevitable rough patches.

Parakeets and the Elderly

When witnessing the loneliness some elderly individuals face, especially after the loss of a spouse or close friend, it's sometimes tempting for family members to run out and buy a pet in an attempt to fill the emotional void. In fact, the image of an "old lady and her budgie" is practically a cliché. Although parakeets can certainly help brighten someone's day with their cheery disposition and clownish antics, think it through before making a rash purchase.

To begin, it's never a good idea to foist a pet onto someone who is unwilling or just plain unenthusiastic about the idea. As mentioned before, budgies are not low maintenance pets! True, they don't need to be walked like a dog or require heavy litter box maintenance like a cat, but they still need daily fresh food and water, attention, and regular cage cleaning. This is where good judgment should come in. The person must not only want the pet, but must also have the wherewithal to care for it. It should be a gift of joy, not an unwelcome physical or financial burden.

If a parakeet will indeed be a welcome addition, then the benefits are many. Numerous studies have shown that elderly pet owners fare significantly better than their pet-less peers in many areas: nutrition, mobility, mood, and even some facets of blood chemistry. That's an awful lot of payback for an investment of a little love and a dish of seeds! In recent years, there's been a strong trend among assisted living centers and Alzheimer's care units to install aviaries within the facilities, and they report that patients are more interactive, calmer, and focused when viewing the birds. For many older people—and, for that matter, for many young ones as well—having a dependent animal that offers unconditional love is the main motivator for getting up in the morning. It's hard to wallow in bed when a cheerful little parakeet is whistling and calling for its breakfast.

Before you move forward with the gift, however, there are a few things you should consider. First of all, buy the bird from a reliable source, and have it checked by an experienced avian veterinarian to make sure it is completely healthy. Although uncommon, there are a few diseases that sick birds can pass on to humans. This is rarely a problem for healthy adults with good immune systems, but an elderly or immune-compromised individual would obviously be at higher risk. Besides, you don't want your loved one to become attached to an unhealthy pet, only to have it die a short while later.

Secondly, if you give a parakeet to a homebound or mobility-restricted person, be sure you provide the cage, food, and all appropriate treats and toys as well. Don't place the burden of acquiring the initial necessities onto a person with limited means to shop for the basics. Depending on the circumstances, it might be necessary for you to continue to supply those items. Some elder care services might provide shopping assistance, but it's unlikely that they will help with pet supplies.

Finally, have a plan in place to re-home the parakeet should the elderly owner pass away or become too ill to maintain a pet. The keet will be grieving from the loss of its owner, and will likely be stressed and fearful from the changes happening around it. If there is another home waiting to accept it with love, it will be a much easier transition for the bird. When human tragedies occur, it's easy to forget that our devoted pets suffer the loss as well.

BUYING A COMPANION PARAKEET

If you can't consistently carve out one hour each day to spend with your parakeet, consider bringing home more than one bird so that your parakeet has a companion and playmate when you're not around.

The decision to add a new pet to your household isn't one that you should take lightly. As mentioned earlier, parakeets can live up to twenty years or more, so your feathered buddy will be dependent upon you for love and attention for a long time. You'll want to start with a young, healthy bird, and give it all the care it needs to thrive. But before that, you will have some more choices to make.

To begin, you should decide just what you expect from your pet, and how much time you expect to spend with it. As mentioned in the last chapter, you should not get a bird (or any pet, for that matter) unless you can commit to spending at least a little quality time with it on a daily basis. Do you want an extremely tame pet that will ride on your shoulder and cuddle, or are you happy to just watch the bird's antics in the cage? Do you want a parakeet that can

talk and do tricks, or will you be just as happy with a less talented companion? Is someone home most days, or are you and your family always on the go? All of these are factors to consider before you make a final decision.

Does Sex Matter?

Because parakeets are intelligent little individuals, it is hard to make sweeping statements about their personality. Neither males nor females make "better" pets. Your best bet is to watch and interact with the birds you're considering, and choose the one that charms you the most. In general, however, there are some characteristics that occur more frequently in one sex or the other. Males are often more gregarious and quick to make friends. Females can be a bit more reserved and cautious around strangers, but once they bond with people, they are devoted and loving. Males are more vocal and will chatter, talk, and sing almost constantly. If you're looking for a bird that will talk, a male might be easier to train. Females can also learn to talk, but they tend to be a little quieter overall. Female parakeets are often bossy and like to rule the roost. Males are usually more easygoing but tend to be hyperactive. Please keep in mind that these are just generalizations, however—there are plenty of exceptions to the rule! Your pet will no doubt have its own unique personality, shaped in part by the love and interest you show it.

One Bird or Two?

If you watch a cage full of juvenile budgies tumbling around like puppies as they play, it will be tempting to buy them all. They seem to be in constant motion: running, flapping, climbing, somersaulting over toys, and squealing with glee—that is, until nap time. Suddenly the chattering stops, and almost at once, they all fluff up and drift off to sleep, ready to start the cycle all over again in a little while. Such is the life of a social flock animal.

When you bring a pet parakeet home, *you* become its flock. If you or other family members have plenty of time to devote each day, it will be fine to keep a single bird. I have seen many patient and affectionate keets riding in toy cars or strolling through dollhouses to the delight of their young owners. On the other hand, if soccer practice and music lessons fill up a big chunk of each day, a single parakeet will be lonely and depressed. These birds require companionship almost as much as they require food and water. If you can't consistently carve out at least an hour a day, consider bringing home more than one bird so that your parakeet has a friend to play with when its human buddies aren't around.

If you are considering multiple birds, make sure that the cage you have is large enough to accommodate them. It should have plenty of room for toys and extra perches to allow the occupants some personal space, just in case they need a little break from all the togetherness. Two males will usually cohabitate nicely, but sometimes multiple females will fight. You can, of course, place a male and female together, but be aware that they might decide to raise a family. Budgies can be quite determined breeders, and the absence of a proper nest box doesn't necessarily deter them. You might find eggs on the cage floor or in food dishes. If this happens, you can either discard the eggs or allow the parents to hatch and rear the chicks. Unless you wish to be in the parakeet breeding business, however, you will need to separate the pair after the chicks are weaned, or babies will continue to "happen." Also, in some cases, same-sex pairs will take on opposite gender roles. In other words, you might see mating attempts between

two males or two females, and on rare occasions two females will begin to lay eggs together. These are obviously infertile and can be discarded.

If you purchase two or more birds at a time, especially if they were already caged together at the pet shop or breeder's facility, you can immediately place them together once you get them home. If, however, you already have a parakeet and wish to get another, you'll have to take some time for introductions. To begin, quarantine the new arrival as discussed in the next chapter. You don't want to expose your existing pet to possible diseases that the new bird could be harboring. If the new parakeet appears healthy after thirty days, or as recom-

mended by your veterinarian, you can move the cages within sight of each other. You will probably notice a lot of back and forth chatter as they introduce themselves. Over the course of a few days, continue to move the cages closer and closer. If the birds are tame enough to come out of their cages, place them on a neutral play area and watch how they behave. In most cases, they will become fast friends.

Once they are comfortable together, you can place them in a new, larger cage. If you plan to use one of the parakeets' current cages to house both, I suggest you first rearrange perches and toys, if possible, in order to cut down on territoriality. If the cage seems a bit different, the original resident will be more interested in exploring the changes than in defending its familiar turf. And, whenever placing birds together for the first time, watch them closely for a few days to make sure they're getting along. Sometimes, one will stake out the food dishes and prevent its cage-mate from eating. If this happens, just place a second set of food and water dishes on the opposite side of the cage. Soon they will learn to share politely.

Colors and Mutations

As you've probably noticed, parakeets are available in a wide variety of beautiful plumage colors in addition to the "wild" or natural green. These color changes happen through a process of genetic mutation, which causes an individual to express a different coloration from its lineage. You are probably familiar with the albinism mutation that causes a lack of pigment in affected individuals, but this is just one of many possible mutations in parakeets.

And surprisingly, the amazing rainbows of feather colors are all produced through a complex interplay of just two pigments! Wild parakeets get their typical green, yellow, and black coloration

from a combination of the pigments eumelanin and psittacofulvin. Eumelanin is responsible for black color, and psittacofulvin is a yellow pigment. When the two are layered and seen in white light (such as sunlight), eumelanin reflects just the blue spectrum of light. As it passes through the yellow psittacofulvin, the human eye perceives it as green. Therefore, a normal green and yellow budgie has areas of pure yellow (just psittacofulvin) and areas of green (psittacofulvin and eumelanin). The black bars and spots are highly concentrated areas of the black pigment. It's easy to understand, therefore, how the complete absence of yellow psittacofulvin pigment results in a bird that is blue and white—if you remove the yellow layers, all that is left are white areas (no pigment), blue areas (eumelanin only), and black markings from concentrated areas of eumelanin. On the other hand, when eumelanin is missing, it results in an all-yellow bird with no traces of blue, green, or black. To simplify, all budgies are divided into two base colors: yellow base birds that express psittacofulvin, and white base birds, in which psittacofulvin is absent.

So far, this might sound pretty straightforward, but nature is rarely that simple. These pigments can combine and rearrange in any number of combinations and densities. There are four basic categories that color mutations fall into:

1. Albinism: In this mutation, eumelanin is either partially or completely reduced in skin, feathers, and eyes. An albino parakeet that is also missing the yellow pigment would appear pure white and would have red eyes due to the lack of eumelanin in the iris of the eye. (Without any pigment, the iris of the eye is clear—the visible blood supply colors the eye red.) If the yellow pigment is present, the bird would be light yellow with red eyes.

2. Dilution: In dilute mutations, eumelanin is partially reduced in only the bird's feathering. These birds can be white or yellow based, but their colors will appear pale and possibly washed out. Their eyes will appear normal.

3. Leucism: In this mutation, both pigments are completely reduced from total or partial areas of skin and feathering, but not the eyes. A bird with total leucism would be pure white, but with normally colored eyes. It is also the mutation responsible for pied feathering, in which case the parakeet has patches of white or colored feathers mixed among otherwise normal markings.

4. Melanism: This condition occurs when eumelanin is increased in the feathering. It will cause feathers to appear darker or alter their hue. As an example, the wild light-green coloration with a melanistic mutation might appear as a dark olive green, and the simple blue (white-based) bird might display as a deep cobalt blue.

As mentioned in the first chapter, there are about thirty-two recognized primary color mutations in budgies, and each of these mutations can combine into a palette of hundreds of different marking and color combinations. In fact, an in-depth look at budgie color genetics could fill an entire book. This brief overview was just intended to help you understand how one little green and yellow bird can now be available in so many different colors. As breeders work to develop new color lines, however, it is possible that other, less desirable

mutations that affect health or longevity can be passed along as well. Some veterinarians and aviculturists have noted a slightly higher incidence of health problems among the more unusual mutations. Keep that in mind when you search for your perfect bird, and don't be too quick to discount the common and familiar green parakeet that charms our Australian neighbors.

Where to Find Parakeets

Unlike their larger parrot cousins, parakeets are commonly available and easy to find. Almost every pet shop, including big-box national chains, will have a selection. In fact, back in the 1950s, parakeets were sold from huge communal cages at dime stores. Unfortunately, they were so ubiquitous that they were sometimes treated as throwaway pets, a cheap toy to appease the children during a shopping outing. Parents could buy a "parakeet kit" that included a too-small cage, a dusty box of seed, a cuttlebone, and a frightened young keet that was stuffed into a cardboard carrier, all for a price less than the fancy train set or talking doll. It's no wonder that they became one of the most popular and common pets in the United States.

Thankfully, times have changed, and most people today are more aware of the responsibilities that come with companion animal ownership. Now, quality pet stores and parakeet breeders usually screen their birds for common diseases and pay stricter attention to their nutritional needs. If you take the time to carefully evaluate a potential seller, you'll be more likely to wind up with a healthy young keet that is well socialized to people and ready to fill a space in your heart. Some good places to find a bird include:

✔ Pet stores. If you choose to buy your parakeet at a pet store, spend some time finding

a store with knowledgeable staff and a wide selection of bird products. The staff can be a valuable resource for answering care questions, and it will be a convenient spot to stock up on food and toys. Make sure the store looks and smells clean, and the animals are housed appropriately. Are the birds being fed a high-quality diet, including some fresh fruits and veggies, and formulated diets? Are the water dishes filled and clean? Do the parakeets have some toys to stimulate them? Do they have enough room to flap their wings and climb around? Don't hesitate to ask questions about their standard of care and any health guarantees that might be available. What happens if the bird becomes ill right after you bring it home?

✔ Parakeet breeders. You might notice classified ads in your local newspaper, or see flyers tacked to bulletin boards in pet supply stores that advertise parakeets for sale. If you choose to deal directly with a breeder, you are likely dealing with someone who has a great deal of specialized experience with the birds. This is a definite plus, but you should use similar standards to judge the breeder's facilities as you use to judge a pet shop. Be aware that most aviculturists will not allow people into the area where the breeding birds are housed, due to concerns about disease transmission and stressing out the parent birds. However, the area where the young birds for sale are housed should be clean and well kept. If you ask to handle a parakeet, the breeder should ask you to wash your hands or use a hand sanitizer first. Don't be put off—this is common sense disease prevention.

✔ Bird fairs. In many towns, local aviculturists stage periodic fairs, where breeders and

suppliers come together to sell live birds and supplies. These can be a wonderful opportunity to see many different types of companion birds and talk with people who have a passion for the parrots and songbirds that line the hall. Unfortunately, it is also an opportunity for diseases to spread, as the stressed birds are temporarily in close proximity to hundreds of others. If you choose to buy a parakeet at a fair, consider purchasing very early in the day, before the bird has been subjected to hundreds of poking fingers from passersby, and be certain you have good contact information for the seller, in case you experience any problems with your new pet after you arrive home.

✔ Previously owned parakeets. Once the word is out that you're looking for a pet parakeet, you might be offered a free or inexpensive bird that a neighbor, friend, or coworker is looking to re-home. This could be an opportunity to get a great pet, or it could be a recipe for heartbreak. To begin, find out why the person is getting rid of the keet. Is it sickly? Untamed and nasty? Neglected and ignored? Sometimes people buy pets on a whim and grow bored once the novelty wears off. These birds, with a little love and attention, can make wonderful pets. If the parakeet is dull and listless, however, it could be health problems that will shorten its life or cost you big money in veterinarian bills. It's often tempting to "rescue" a neglected or sickly pet, but be aware that this can be an expensive act of kindness.

Finding an Avian Veterinarian

Before you bring a parakeet into your home, you should do some research and find a veterinarian to care for your pet. Don't be fooled into thinking that your usual dog or cat veterinarian will be qualified to work on birds; pet birds are nothing at all like canines, felines, or other small mammals. Avian veterinarians are specialists who spend some or all of their time working on feathered patients. Many avian practices also see other exotic animals, such as reptiles and amphibians, but few veterinarians are able to offer care for the entire gamut of companion animals; that's why they specialize.

To find an avian veterinarian, ask the breeder or pet shop for a recommendation. If they sell birds, they should have a good working relationship with a qualified veterinarian. (If they don't, then that is a major red flag—consider buying your parakeet elsewhere.) You can also ask your dog/cat veterinarian for a referral, or contact the Association of Avian Veterinarians at *www. aav.org* for a list of members in your area.

As soon as you purchase your parakeet, you should bring it in for a new bird "wellness check." Your veterinarian might have a package price for exams and testing, and he or she can discuss what tests or future exams might need to be scheduled. Be aware that sellers who issue a health guarantee usually require that you have the bird examined by a veterinarian within a certain time frame, or the guarantee is voided.

Before you choose an avian veterinarian, spend a little time familiarizing yourself with the clinic. Here are some questions to ask:

✔ How many birds does the practice see in a week? Are birds the primary specialty?

✔ Is the veterinarian a member of the Association of Avian Veterinarians (AAV)? Although there are excellent practitioners who do not maintain membership in AAV, membership in this specialized group does indicate someone who is serious about bird care.

✔ Are the clinic's hours compatible with your schedule? Few veterinary hospitals have late evening hours every day, but one evening a week or some Saturday hours might make it more convenient to get your pet in for routine visits.

✔ How does the veterinarian handle after-hours emergencies? In my experience, my pet birds only get sick or hurt on extended holiday weekends when there isn't a veterinarian left in the entire state. Be sure that your chosen vet has an emergency contact available. If emergencies are referred to a local animal emergency hospital, ask if the emergency clinic has avian experience.

✔ Is the veterinarian willing to work within your financial constraints? Some practices might allow you to make payments over time if you are honestly unable to afford an unexpected emergency. However, if you cannot afford routine care, it might be best to wait until your finances improve before you take on the responsibility of a new pet.

HOW-TO: CHOOSING A

The first step in choosing a healthy keet is to observe it from a distance. Birds are prey animals, and they will do everything in their power to hide illness or injury and keep up with the flock. If a sick bird knows you are watching it, it will attempt to appear normal and healthy. Instead, find a spot where you see the bird, but it can't easily see you. Watch carefully, and be aware of the following points:

✔ Posture and movement. A healthy parakeet will appear alert and rambunctious. It will move around easily, and be quick to climb and flap its wings. Avoid a bird that appears lethargic, lame, or reluctant to move. A sleepy bird might tuck its head under its feathers for a short nap, but a bird that buries its head in its feathers for an extended period during the day, or seems slow to rouse, might very well be sick.

✔ Feathers. A healthy parakeet has nearly 3,000 feathers that keep it warm, allow it to fly, act as camouflage, and help to attract a mate. Feathers should be smooth, bright, and held closely to the body. A budgie with feathers that are dull, fluffed, or missing in patches is probably not healthy. Birds will commonly fluff their feathers when cold or sleepy, but a healthy bird will tighten its feathers as soon as it wakes from its nap or begins to move around. In young parakeets, missing or broken feathers—especially tail feathers—can be simply a result of rough play with cagemates, but they can also signify disease or parasites. Be especially wary of young-sters with feathers that appear deformed or clubbed, as this can be a sign of seri-ous disease.

✔ Eyes. The eyes should be bright, alert, and free of dis-charge or swellings. A bird with dull, listless eyes is likely very sick. Young budgies have bright, black, "shoe-button" eyes, which lighten as they get older. By the time the bird is about eight months old, the irises are a medium to light grey.

✔ Signs of discomfort. A bird that constantly rubs its face on a perch, or that pumps its tail up and down as it breathes, is probably suffer-ing from a respiratory disease. Other respiratory warning signs include open-mouthed breathing, nasal or ocular dis-charge, frequent head shak-ing, sneezing, or a clicking sound as the bird breathes. Other signs of discomfort, such as picking at feathers,

HEALTHY PARAKEET

frequent scratching and poking at the skin, or frantic pacing interspersed with scratching might indicate parasites. This is not to be confused with normal preening and grooming, which a healthy bird will do in a relaxed manner before it moves on to other activities.

After you've observed from a distance, you can do a hands-on check. Gently pick up the keet, and take a closer look at its eyes, nostrils, and beak, which should all be clean and free of discharge or injury. The legs, feet, and toes should be well scaled but smooth, and free of any sores or inflamed areas. Next, check the bird's weight. The easiest way to do this is to examine the keel bone, which is the breastbone that runs down the center of a bird's chest. A healthy parakeet should be evenly muscled with a smooth chest. On an overweight bird, you will barely be able to feel the bone. If a bird is underweight, the bone will feel prominent, almost sharp. Never buy an underweight bird, because weight loss is one of the first signs of disease. Look under the tail to observe its vent area, which should be clean and free of pasted feces. If the bird's vent feathers are wet or dirty, it might indicate gastrointestinal disease or parasites.

Finally, consider how the parakeet has reacted to your handling. Is it friendly and alert, not lethargic or listless? Does it appear interested in you, or is it unhappy about being held? If it appears healthy but is nervous and slightly reluctant to be held, it can be a good pet if you're willing to invest some time to earn its trust. Avoid a bird that is frantic and terrified of handling, however, even if it appears healthy. Some birds just don't have the personality or desire for human companionship, especially if they were poorly socialized out of the nest. These parakeets can likely be tamed, but it will involve quite a time commitment and a lot of patience. Of course, if a bird displays any of the signs of illness listed above, do not purchase it with the hope that it will get better under your care. Although that is certainly possible, an already ill bird faced with the stress of moving to a new home has an awful lot going against it. Point out your concerns to the pet shop or breeder, and look elsewhere to find a healthy pet that will be around to share your life for a long time.

BRINGING HOME YOUR PET

Make sure to set up a cage and supplies before you bring your new parakeet home. This will ensure a smooth and stress-free transition for both you and your new bird!

All too often, new parakeet owners make the mistake of buying a cage, supplies, and bird all at the same time. They come home, sometimes with noisy and excited children in tow, and rush to put everything together while the stressed-out bird huddles in terror in a small, dark cardboard carrier. Trust me; this is not the way to do it.

In order to make the transition to a new home as painless as possible for your parakeet, plan in advance and have everything ready before you pick up your new pet. If children will share in the bird's care, now is the time to discuss specific chores and responsibilities. Take the time to think about proper cage placement, food storage, and who will care for your parakeet if you travel. Gather information on local avian veterinarians in case your pet becomes ill. If you already have other pet birds, be aware that you will need to quarantine the new arrival for at least thirty days to watch for illnesses that might be contagious; decide on a quarantine area and discuss proper handling methods with other family members. We'll discuss all of these things in more detail throughout the book, but the point is that it's best to prepare *before* you bring a new pet into your home. It will be less stressful for the bird *and* for you!

Choosing a Cage

Because parakeets are such popular companions, most pet stores carry a wide variety of cages purportedly designed for birds of their size. Be aware, though, that not all cages are suitable, no matter what the manufacturer claims. To begin, you must realize that the cage you choose will be your budgie's home for a long time, and it should be comfortable and roomy. Think of it this way: would you rather spend your life crammed into a small studio apartment, or in a spacious and airy home? Your bird will feel much the same way. A too-small cage will not allow your pet enough room to explore, play, and exercise properly. I recommend a cage that is at least 18 inches (46 cm) in each dimension. Surprisingly, the cage height is the least important dimension. Although parakeets do enjoy climbing, fly-ing is the best exercise. A long rectangular cage allows the bird to flap its wings and fly a short distance across the cage. Very tall but narrow rectangular cages (which are actually quite common) are not a good choice, as they make it impossible for the bird to fly. And avoid round cages—these do not allow the keet to retreat to a safe corner when it feels threatened, and they are rarely wide enough for flight. Always purchase the largest and longest cage your budget will allow. Not only will your bird be happier, but it will likely be healthier from the increased physical activity. Be sure that the larger cage is designed for small birds, however, and does not have widely spaced bars. You do not want a cage that will allow your bird to stick its head out. A curious parakeet might force its head between the bars and then twist and get stuck or strangle itself. For keets, bar spacing of no more than ½ inch (1.3 cm) is safest.

Once you narrow your search down to a few cages of appropriate size and shape, take a closer look at the cage features. Here are some other considerations:

✔ Which direction do the bars run? Horizontal bars are easiest for climbing but are more likely to collect poop. Many cages today have hori-zontal bars on two sides, and vertical on the other two. This is a nice compromise between utility and convenience.

✔ How large is the cage door, and how does it open? Larger doors allow you more access for servicing the cage but also make it easier for your pet to bolt past you and escape. Some cages feature a small door inside a larger one, which you can open according to your need. Avoid "guillotine" style lift-up doors. Some parakeets love to repetitively lift and drop these, which is annoying and creates a safety issue should the bird become trapped under-neath. The best types are either fold-down "landing" style doors, or swing-out doors.

✔ How is the cage made? Sturdy wire and metal is the best material. For a parakeet-sized cage, it's likely that the base might be made of plastic, but choose the heaviest and highest-quality available. Cheap plastic will warp, stain, and crack quickly, making that bargain cage not such a bargain in the long run. Run your hand across the surfaces to check for sharp or uneven points that might pose a danger. All-acrylic cages might be appealing, but they tend to get scratched and hazy after a while, and they won't allow your pet to climb around for exercise. Never put your parakeet in a wooden, bamboo, or decorative cage of any sort. These aren't intended to house live birds and might contain toxins. Besides, an industrious budgie will quickly gnaw through wood and escape.

✔ How many food and water dishes does the cage hold? You will want one that holds at least three dishes: water, dry food, and fresh food. If possible, buy an extra set or two of replacement dishes. That way, you can run the dirty ones through the dishwasher (or wash by hand) and always have a clean set avail-able. The best types are stainless steel or heavy plastic. Galvanized metal cups can leach toxic metals—don't use them. Cheap, lightweight

plastic will crack and discolor and require frequent replacement, and ceramic can crack and harbor germs. Avoid hooded cups, because some budgies are fearful of putting their head into a covered dish and might refuse to eat or drink from them. High-quality dishes are worth a little extra money.

✔ Do the doors and feeder doors open smoothly without catching and dragging? Does the bottom tray pull out easily? If you have to wrestle with the cage each time you clean it, it will quickly become an unpleasant nuisance. Is there a wire grate over the bottom tray so that you can remove the tray without your bird escaping?

✔ Does the cage come with a stand, or will you have to place it on furniture? If it has a stand, make sure it is sturdy enough to withstand bumping by kids or pets without toppling over.

✔ What kinds of perches are included? The plain round wooden dowels or plastic perches that come with many cages are not a good choice and should be discarded. These hard uniform surfaces create pressure points on the bird's feet and can cause sores. The best perch is a natural wood branch of varying thicknesses and with angled branches. This helps to flex and exercise the keet's foot muscles and can improve balance and grip. You can find these in most pet stores, or create your own. If you do cut your own branches, be certain the wood you choose is not toxic, and scrub it thoroughly in hot soapy water (rinse and dry

completely) before you place it in your bird's cage. Rope and cement perches are also fine to add as additional perching surfaces. The key is to provide variety in diameter and texture.

Cage Location

Before you bring home your new pet, you will need to decide where it will fit in your home. Parakeets are social creatures, and they will be very unhappy if they are stuffed into a rarely used back room. On the other hand, placing the cage in the middle of the highest traffic spot might be stressful for the bird, as it has to tolerate a constant parade of people and pets while it is trying to rest. The ideal spot is in a secure corner of a room that the owner frequents, such as a family room or den.

(Kitchens, however, are poor choices because fumes from cooking or cleaning can be lethal to birds.) In any case, position the cage so that the bird can see and interact with family members, yet be shielded from roughhousing kids or dogs. Place the cage high enough so that the bird doesn't have to fend off curious noses or paws from other pets. Typically, dogs will get used to and learn to ignore a feathered companion pretty quickly, but cats and ferrets have a harder time overcoming their predatory instincts.

Although your bird will likely enjoy looking out the window, make sure you don't place the cage directly in front of a sunny window where it can overheat. Always allow at least a portion of the cage to remain shaded. And be aware that although your parakeet might have

Outdoor Safety Tips

If you want to bring your parakeet outdoors, know how to avoid dangers and risks that can turn the outing into a tragedy:

• Never allow your bird out of its cage when it is outside. Even a bird with carefully clipped wings can climb, flutter, or jump into trouble.

• Do not leave your parakeet unattended outdoors, even if it is safely caged. Predators such as cats, raccoons, snakes, and hawks can tip or open a cage, and your pet will be defenseless.

• Make sure that the cage isn't in direct sunlight, and that the bird has a shady place to retreat if it gets too warm.

• Do not allow your bird access to outdoor grass, plants, or soil. Wild animals and birds can carry diseases and parasites that can infect pet birds, and these pathogens can live in the soil or on foliage. Instead, offer your keet washed fresh greens, or grow a dish of grass seed indoors to offer as a treat.

• Your parakeet might welcome a gentle shower from a mister bottle or fine hose spray while outside. Always point the sprayer up and let the water fall softly—do not point the nozzle directly at the bird. Make sure it is enjoying the process, and stop immediately if the bird appears stressed or frightened. And after the shower, dry cage surfaces thoroughly to prevent mold growth.

fun watching small finches congregate near an outside feeder, the appearance of hawks or owls will terrify your pet and might cause it to thrash and injure itself. Use common sense if you live in an area that is rife with raptors.

Air Quality

It should come as no surprise that fresh air and natural light have plenty of health-enhancing benefits. We have all probably experienced the feeling of stepping outside on the first glorious spring day and feeling the breeze in our face and the sun on our skin. How can you duplicate these benefits for your indoor bird? Although it is fine to haul your pet's cage outdoors occasionally, it's important to consider the air and light quality inside your home.

Our indoor air—especially in well-insulated homes—contains an unappetizing blend of pollutants and germs. Healthy people with no respiratory problems might never notice, but folks with allergies or asthma are usually all too well aware of the challenges. When you bring a pet bird into the home, it will contribute its own mix of molted feathers, dander, and aerosolized feces. That's why a high-quality air purifier is an important investment. Cleaner air will benefit not just your pet, but your family as well.

The best air purifiers use HEPA filtration, which is an acronym for "High-Efficiency Particulate Air." These filters were developed to capture stray radioactive particles by scientists working on the Manhattan Project in the 1940s, so they are quite able to clear the air of something as simple as bird dander! Because HEPA filters are somewhat pricey, many manufacturers include carbon pre-filters that remove most of the bigger gunk from the air before it reaches the HEPA filter. The carbon pre-filters can be washed or replaced with ease, which will prolong the life of the more expensive filter. If you purchase one of these units, make sure that it is appropriately sized for the room in which you're using it. You will

30 and 50 percent. If the humidity is too low, the dry air can crack skin, dull hair, aggravate respiratory problems, and create an unpleasant buildup of static electricity. Those of us in northern states are well aware of this phenomenon during the winter, when the blazing furnace sucks available moisture from the air. At these times, a good humidifier will keep you and your parakeet comfortable and more resistant to respiratory infections. On the other hand, too much humidity—think of southern states during hot, wet weather—can promote the growth of mold and mildew, including some pathogens that also cause disease. During these spells, a dehumidifier can bring the moisture levels back down into a comfortable and healthy range.

The Right Light

In our industrialized society, many of us spend the bulk of our time indoors under artificial lighting. Of course, we have the ability to walk outside and enjoy some natural sunlight. Your parakeet doesn't have that choice. That's why you should make your indoor lighting as healthful as possible, for your benefit and for your pet.

In recent decades, scientists have learned a lot about how natural light affects living creatures. Sunlight affects our hormones, impacts our body rhythms, and even helps us synthesize some vitamins. Although some of these effects are triggered by visible light, much of the magic of sunshine is contained in its invisible ultraviolet (UV) rays. UV light is classified into three categories, depending on the length of the light wave: UVA, UVB, and UVC. In the past, researchers focused mainly on the

need to know the approximate cubic footage of the area to make an informed decision. For example, if the room is 12 feet (3.7 m) by 15 feet (4.6 m), with 9 foot (2.7 m) ceilings, you would require a unit that is large enough to purify 1620 cubic feet (45.9 m^3). If the device is too small, it will not be able to process the air with enough frequency, but an expensive, oversized unit will not clean the air any more thoroughly than a properly sized one.

Although clean air is important, it is also important to maintain a proper humidity level indoors. Most people (and pets) will feel best when the relative humidity is between role of UVB on human skin; it is the light that causes sunburn, but it also helps our bodies create vitamin D. Now we know that UVA and UVC can also cause damage through different mechanisms. Although UV rays are undoubtedly dangerous in excess, triggering skin cancer and damaging exposed skin, we need at least some brief exposure to remain healthy.

The same is true for your parakeet. Some folks address this need by placing the cage near a window so that their pet can bathe in sunbeams. Although this will supply the visual stimulation of natural light, window glass blocks more than 90 percent of UVB and UVC rays, and a lesser portion of UVA. To compensate, many pet bird enthusiasts recommend using full-spectrum lighting around bird cages. In theory, these special bulbs mimic the range of light waves emitted by the sun, including the UV ranges. Unfortunately, there is no regulation among lighting manufacturers to standardize the meaning of "full-spectrum," and the available models sometimes differ greatly in their output. Although there seems to be little scientific proof that these lights actually work, there's plenty of anecdotal evidence to

support them. I have used them over the years, and I believe they keep my birds healthier and happier. Just buy a quality brand, preferably from a manufacturer that specifically targets the bird community, and follow their instructions for placement and usage.

Temperature

People who have heard the frequent admonition to keep pet birds safe from drafts often assume that our feathered companions are like hothouse orchids, and that they require very warm temperatures in order to thrive. Actually, that isn't true at all. Although your parakeet will be happiest at normal room temperature, wild keets in Australia face temperature extremes that can range from below freezing to more than 120°F (49°C). They are hardy and adaptive little birds! The key is to avoid sudden temperature fluctuations, which can stress them and weaken their immune system. Use common sense, and place the cage out of range from heating and air conditioning vents and away from frequently opened doors in the winter. Cold drafts or warm blasts won't usually harm the bird directly, but the shock will make it more susceptible to illnesses.

Quarantine

As mentioned earlier in this chapter, you must quarantine your new parakeet if you already have other pet birds in the house. This will help to protect both your existing birds and the new arrival from hidden diseases and infections. Even a healthy looking bird can be a latent carrier of disease. What this means is that the bird carries an illness that does not normally make it sick, but it can transmit the illness to others. During times of stress, such as moving to a new home or welcoming a new member to the flock, the illness might flare up and sicken its host, or spread to other susceptible species. That's why quarantine is so important. It will give your parakeet a chance to slowly settle in and give you a chance to further evaluate its health.

True quarantine is a complicated and precise procedure that requires consideration of factors such as shared airflow in a dwelling, and it would be very difficult to achieve in an average household. A basic home quarantine isn't as foolproof but is much simpler and will provide at least some protection from disease transmission. To begin, situate the new bird in a room as far away as possible from the other birds. This will just be a temporary location (about thirty days or as recommended by your veterinarian), so a rarely used back bedroom is fine. If possible, close heating and air conditioning vents that might draw dander throughout the house. If this is not possible, running a HEPA purifier in the room will cleanse the air as it circulates and make it less likely that pathogens will travel far and wide. If weather permits, you can crack open a window for ventilation.

Always feed and clean the quarantined bird last, and wash your hands thoroughly between cages. It's also a good idea to change clothes before handling your existing pets again. Wash any sponges or cleaning implements in hot soapy water, and do not let children or dogs and cats run in and out of the quarantine room, thus tracking possible pathogens in or out of the room. If you see any signs of illness in the birds, contact an avian veterinarian immediately. Otherwise, after about thirty days it should be safe to move the new keet to its permanent spot among the rest of your flock.

These recommendations might sound harsh and difficult, but you will be risking the health of your birds if you ignore them. Even a strict thirty-day quarantine is no guarantee of safety—some latent diseases can surface after years of apparent health—but at least you will be likely to detect any obvious problems during the month.

DIET FOR A HEALTHY PARAKEET

A healthy parakeet diet consists of whole grains, seeds, veggies, and fruit.

Back in the old days when companion bird nutrition was an unknown science, feeding a pet parakeet seemed uncomplicated. You simply walked into your local grocery store, pet store, or five-and-dime store and purchased a small cardboard box that was clearly labeled "parakeet seed." The boxes—and the seeds they contained—were often dusty and sometimes contaminated with tiny insects, but the picture of the perky and happy bird on the front panel assured the purchasers that they were buying a quality diet. Add a cuttlebone, some gravel-coated cage paper, and a dish of water, and your bird was all set.

Thankfully, we have come a long way since then. Our knowledge of avian nutrition has grown by leaps and bounds, although we still have much to learn about the needs of individual species. One thing we have learned, however, is that malnutrition is the number-one cause of pet bird deaths. Does that surprise you? If it does, it's because most of us confuse malnutrition with starvation or food deprivation. In truth, it is often our overfed, sometimes obese pets that are suffering from chronic diseases linked directly to poor diet. As humans, we've become aware of the correlation between high-fat, high-sodium, and high-sugar processed foods and our current health crisis of diabetes, cancer, and coronary disease. And yet many people fail to link the same causes to the deteriorating health of their pets.

Malnutrition is a sneaky killer. It rarely kills directly, but instead weakens an organism and suppresses (or overexcites) immune function, creating a cascade of chemical changes that open the door to disease and inflammation. Parakeets are especially prone to fatty tumors, liver and kidney disease, gout, and thyroid problems that are all caused or exacerbated by poor diet. And all too often, the standard American keet diet of seed alone is the culprit.

In the wild, budgies are nomadic, traveling long distances to follow the food supply. They eat a wide variety of plant materials, feasting on various seeding grasses, weeds, and flowering plants during the wet season, and subsisting on desert scrub grasses during dry months. That is how the concept took hold that captive parakeets would thrive on a seed diet. What was lost in translation, however, is an understanding of the massive nutritional differences between a wild diet and one comprised of cultivated seed and grain.

The typical keet mix sold for pet birds usually consists of a small variety of different millet seeds, some canary grass seed, and maybe oat groats and a few other ingredients. Some premium mixes add bits of dried greens and vegetables. Although there's nothing wrong with these mixes, they are not a complete diet. In general, they are too high in fat and deficient in key nutrients, especially vitamins A and D, some amino acids, and calcium. Many

Nutritional Profile of Commonly Fed Seeds

Note: Values are approximate and will vary according to soil conditions, water availability, weather, and other factors.
✔ White Proso Millet: 3.5% fat, 12% protein, 64% carbohydrates
✔ Foxtail (Spray) Millet: 4% fat, 11% protein, 63% carbohydrates
✔ Canary Grass Seed: 5.5% fat, 16.5% protein, 52% carbohydrates
✔ Hulled Oats (Oat Groats): 7% fat, 12.5% protein, 67% carbohydrates
✔ Wheat: 2% fat, 11.5% protein, 71% carbohydrates
✔ Flax Seed: 34.5% fat, 23% protein, 30% carbohydrates

manufacturers "vitamin-enrich" the mixes by adding fortified pellets or using a vitamin spray on the seeds, but it's questionable how much of the vitamins actually make it into the bird. Parakeets hull seeds before eating them, so the vitamin-enriched husk simply gets discarded, and the fortified pellets do no good if they get tossed aside in favor of the tasty seed.

Contrast this captive dry seed diet to the native vegetation consumed by wild birds: researchers have identified over 130 varieties of seeding wild grasses in Australia that provide a source of food to budgies. The green seeds and buds form while the plants are bursting from the ground during the rainy season. Australia's soil is generally high in minerals due to its past as a shallow tropical sea, and many of the plants act as nutrient pumps, drawing valuable substances such as calcium and iron into the seeds. And, besides the wide

array of available grasses and weeds, wild keets also consume cultivated grains from the farms spread across the land. As you can see, this is a far cry from a box of dusty seeds!

The Basics

What, then, is a healthy parakeet diet? You might be surprised to hear that it is actually very similar to what health-conscious humans eat: lots of whole grains, veggies, and fruit. It isn't as complicated as it might sound; if you provide a quality base diet, your pet can share many of your foods to cover all its nutritional needs. Unfortunately, parakeets—like kids— often prefer tasty "junk" food to healthier alternatives. With a few tricks and a little per-

sistence, however, you can convince your keet to eat like a champ.

To begin, you must decide on a basic daily diet. Here's where the aforementioned seed mixes come in, although there are other alternatives. Pet food manufacturers now offer a wide variety of formulated diets for birds. Commonly referred to as "pellets," these diets are the bird equivalents of dry dog or cat food. They're made with ground and cooked seeds and grains, which are extruded or pressed into species-appropriate sizes and shapes. They contain all the known necessary vitamins and minerals and often include other ingredients such as probiotics, flavors, and colors. Pellets, like seed, can vary in quality from manufacturer to manufacturer, so don't hesitate to ask

for recommendations from your avian veterinarian. You can choose to use only pellets for a base diet, only seed mixes, or a combination of the two. Keep in mind, however, that foods are only healthy if they're eaten. If you supply your pet with large dishes of seeds and pellets, it might pick and choose favorite bits and ignore the rest. It's better to feed smaller amounts more frequently, which will encourage more balanced eating habits.

Whatever you choose, buy the best and the freshest in the smallest practicable quantities. Pellets should have a "best by" date on the package, and some premium seed mixes also carry freshness dates. Try to shop at stores that

have a high turnover of food, and be wary of bulk bins that make it impossible to judge the age or quality of feed. Although it might seem like a smart idea to stock up, you will run the risk of food getting rancid or becoming infested with insects. Not only is spoiled seed less nutritious, but it might be harboring invisible mycotoxins from fungus and mold that are extremely dangerous to your bird. Many bird care books advise smelling, sprouting, or even tasting the seed to see if it's fresh, but this can be misleading. Although obviously rancid or musty-smelling seed is always dangerous and should be discarded, sometimes perfectly fresh and clean-smelling seed is still contaminated

The Parakeet Palate

I've often had birds that refuse a novel food for weeks, even months, and then one day suddenly give it a try and decide they like it. Your keet might be more willing to try new foods if it first sees you (or another bird) eating the item. You can show the food to the bird, and then eat some yourself, making an obvious show of pleasure: "Mmmm, this is *good!* Yum!" If it appears interested, offer a piece. It might not sample it right away, but after a few times its curiosity will likely win out. I have a Timneh African grey that will eat anything—edible or not—that is placed in her food dish. She is a great "food model" for the other birds and has influenced many to expand their palates.

and unsafe. Your best bet is to purchase in small quantities from trusted manufacturers and suppliers. Some brands are now packaged in bags that are flushed with nitrogen or carbon dioxide before they are sealed. This flushing removes air, kills any insect larvae that might be present, prevents the growth of molds, and preserves the freshness of the seed for a much longer time.

Dry Food Storage

Once you get the food home, store it in an airtight container in a cool, dry location. It's fine to freeze or refrigerate seed to keep it fresh longer, but be careful to avoid condensation caused by rapid temperature changes, because moisture can spur the growth of mold. In general, air and water (and, to a lesser degree, light) are all enemies of seed, causing

it to decay or turn rancid at a rapid rate. If you buy in reasonable quantities, however, and store it properly, you shouldn't have any issues. The same advice holds true for formulated diets, although these usually contain some preservatives—either natural or artificial—that make them slightly less vulnerable to storage problems.

Insects and Rodents

Bird seed and pellets are not attractive only to your parakeet; they also look yummy to a wide variety of pests, including grain beetles, seed moths, and mice. Again, careful storage and regular cage cleaning can help you avoid many of these problems. If you do experience an infestation, you must first identify the culprit. Mice are obvious. Signs of mice include droppings, gnawed items, squeaking sounds, and grease or dirt trails along walls or furniture. They can be difficult to control, and mouse poison poses a great threat to children and pets. Traps are a safer alternative, but place them in areas where curious pets won't get an unpleasant surprise. A snapped mouse trap might be painful or frightening to a dog or cat, but it could be lethal to your parakeet. If mice gain access to any pet food, discard it immediately. Rodents carry many diseases that can infect animals, birds, and humans. A veterinarian or doctor bill will quickly outweigh any savings from salvaged feed—so be sure to discard any food that could have been contaminated by rodents.

Insects, on the other hand, are more of an annoyance than a threat. The two most common types attracted to pet foods are seed moths and grain beetles. Seed moths are often called pantry moths, flour moths, Mediterranean flour moths, or Indian grain moths. They are small, brownish, flying insects that you might see fluttering around pantry staples, including grains, dried beans, dried fruit, cereal, and of course pet food. The adult female lays eggs in a food source, where the larvae hatch and begin to feed. At this stage, they look like small (1/2 inch, or 1.3 cm) off-white or yellowish caterpillars. Once the larvae eat and develop, they begin to spin webs for their cocoons. Often, the first sign of contaminated seed is a layer of sticky webbing around the container. In a few weeks, the pupae emerge from their cocoons as adults and the cycle begins again. When you buy bird food in plastic bags, never buy a bag that feels sticky or has visible webbing; it's a likely sign that seed moths are present.

To prevent or kill moths, place any susceptible foods in the freezer for at least four days, which should kill any adults or larvae. Eggs are sometimes more resistant but will not hatch if the food is kept frozen or refrigerated. Don't worry if your parakeet does eat seed that is contaminated with insects. The bugs aren't harmful and actually can provide some additional protein, as unappetizing as that might sound. However, buggy seed can also indicate that the product is old or has been poorly stored, so be on the lookout for other signs of deterioration.

Another common pantry pest is the grain beetle, or the grain weevil. There are numerous species of these tiny black or dark brown beetles, and they infest grains, seeds, flours, and many other foods. They most commonly appear as a flat oval speck, about the size of an alfalfa seed. As in the case of the seed moths, preven-

To Sprout or Not?

One healthy food that's often recommended for pet birds is sprouted seeds. There are many different types on the market, from tiny and tart radish sprouts through the familiar mung bean sprouts used in Chinese cooking. All sprouts are dynamos of nutrition, filled with protein, vitamins, and enzymes. You can purchase them in grocery stores, or sprout your own seeds at home. Unfortunately, sprouts are also quite fragile and prone to contamination and spoilage. In fact, the Food and Drug Administration and Centers for Disease Control have issued dire warnings about the dangers of consuming raw sprouts after several deadly outbreaks of salmonella were linked to their consumption. If you do wish to feed sprouts, consider lightly cooking them first to kill dangerous pathogens.

tion is the best defense. These bugs typically chew tiny holes in bags or boxes of food, which might be visible on very close inspection. Grain beetles don't fly, but you might see them scurry deep into a suspect food when disturbed. Freezing works to control these as well. Because I find them a little harder to eradicate and more invasive than seed moths, I typically discard any pet food they contaminate. Again, they are not dangerous to ingest, so feel free to toss any infested seed out to the wild birds.

Fresh Foods

Although we've spent a lot of time discussing base diets, please don't think that any seed mix—or even a high-quality formulated diet—will provide 100 percent nutrition. Your pet needs a variety of fresh foods to round out its diet. Parakeets aren't usually adventurous eaters and might need some convincing to try new foods, but the reward will be increased health and a longer life. The key is persistence.

Because budgies can't hold food in their feet like other parrots, be sure that the food is cut to an appropriate size. Chop fruits and veggies into small pieces, or wedge larger chunks tightly between the cage bars so that your keet can gnaw on them. Many parakeets enjoy taking a bath by rolling around on wet leafy greens, so try placing a few large wet leaves of romaine lettuce or kale on a dish on the cage floor—once bath time is over, the bird is likely to take a few nibbles. Visual creatures like parrots are also intrigued by interesting shapes, colors, and textures. Offer broccoli buds,

matchstick cut carrots, or the ruby red and juicy pomegranate arils (seeds). Some pet supply stores sell stainless steel hanging skewers, which will allow you to create a healthy bird shish kebab of various fruits and veggies.

Almost all fruits and vegetables are safe for birds, with the exception of avocado. Parts of the avocado contain a toxic fatty acid derivative called persin. Although it is found primarily in the leaves, bark, and pit, birds are highly sensitive to even trace amounts of persin and can suffer respiratory or cardiac failure if they ingest any. Keep avocados, avocado plants, and foods such as guacamole far away from your pet. Onions, garlic, and sweet peas have also been associated with possible toxicities when consumed in large quantities, so use these with caution. A little onion or garlic as seasoning certainly won't hurt (and might even have

health benefits), but don't let your keet munch on a wedge of raw onion or eat a whole garlic clove, even if it is so inclined.

You will likely encounter long lists of supposedly toxic food items on the Internet, but many of these are incorrect or misinformed. For example, eggplant and tomato leaves are toxic, but the fruit is perfectly safe. Some folks claim that budgies should not be allowed to eat certain veggies, such as cauliflower, kale, and cabbage. The reasoning behind this advice is that some vegetables, especially those in the *Brassica* family, are considered goitrogenic. In simple terms, in raw form these plants contain substances that hamper the thyroid's ability to utilize iodine. Because parakeets are prone

Foods to Avoid
✔ Avocado*
✔ Chocolate*
✔ Caffeine*
✔ Alcohol*
✔ Onions, garlic, and peas in large quantities
✔ Dried beans* (cooked are healthy)
✔ Raw cruciferous vegetable (cooked are healthy)
✔ Dairy products (small quantities are safe)
✔ Salty, sugary, or high-fat treats*
✔ "Empty" calories from refined grains and processed foods*

Note that this may not be a complete list. Certain items, such as peas and garlic, are possibly safe. Some experts disagree on the potential danger. Items marked with an asterisk, however, are indisputably dangerous.

to iodine deficiencies and thyroid problems, it stands to reason that these foods could be harmful.

Cooking, however, inactivates the substances, and these same vegetables are nutritional powerhouses. Feel free to offer these foods to your pet—in moderation if raw, and in abundance if you take the time to cook them first. In reality, most cases of thyroid disease are caused or exacerbated by a poor diet that consists of seed alone, not a diet that contains healthy whole foods. If your keet is suffering from an iodine deficiency, there are iodine supplements that can be added to the drinking water, but don't use them except under the advice of a veterinarian. Although iodine toxicity is rare, it can occur.

Cooked Diets and People Food

Another healthy dietary option is cooked grains and beans. There are many brands of cooking diets now on the market for pet birds, and they usually contain a blend of rice and grains, dried fruits or veggies, beans, and spices. You can purchase small bags to see what your bird prefers, or create your own. It doesn't have to be fancy; for example, many keets love to share their owner's morning oatmeal. If you go easy on the sugar and add some chopped nuts and fruit, it will be a breakfast you both can enjoy. Just be careful to cook grains and beans before feeding—dried, uncooked beans contain a trypsin inhibitor that interferes with protein metabolism. Once they are thoroughly cooked, however, they are a great source of protein and trace minerals.

As you experiment with different foods, you'll probably discover that tame parakeets often want to eat what you're eating, and if you eat healthy foods, feel free to share! Of course, the key word here is "healthy." Brown rice, whole grain pasta, cooked vegetables, and bits of pizza (crust and tomato sauce) are often favored treats. Do not feed your pet junk food like candy or chips. Although a single bite of a potato chip probably won't cause abrupt harm, frequent access to salty, sugary, fatty, and nutritionally empty foods definitely will endanger your pet's health. And, some of your vices could be immediately lethal—chocolate, alcohol, nicotine, and caffeine are deadly to birds. If you smoke, don't do it near your bird, and scrub your hands thoroughly before picking up the keet. Nicotine residue on your fingers can cause severe dermatitis on your budgie's feet.

Foods to Feed

These foods are nutritional powerhouses, and often very attractive to parakeets:
✔ Broccoli florets (lightly cooked is best)
✔ Cooked sweet potato
✔ Blueberries
✔ Pomegranate arils (seeds)
✔ Kale
✔ Shredded carrots
✔ Cooked pumpkin or other winter squash
✔ Cooked oatmeal
✔ Hard-boiled egg yolk
✔ Kiwi fruit
✔ Cooked whole grain pasta

Remember, your pet might not sample an unfamiliar food on the first—or even the fifteenth—attempt. Keep offering bits of healthy food, and one day you might be surprised to see your keet munching happily away.

Treats

Offering treats is a great way to reward your parakeet and create a bond. Although treats can be a little indulgent, don't let your pet become a treat junkie that is habituated to high-fat, sugary goodies. Pet stores offer aisles and aisles of cage bird treats in various shapes, colors, and sizes. For many years, most of these consisted of various seeds cemented together with molasses or honey and untold other ingredients. The budgie seed bell—a bell-shaped glob of seed and sugars with a tiny cowbell attached—became an almost iconic fixture in parakeet cages across America. There's nothing wrong with occasionally offering such a delight, but don't make it a daily habit.

Another budgie favorite is millet spray. The seeding heads of foxtail or finger millet are cut and dried whole to provide an entertaining and relatively healthy snack for birds. It's quite entertaining to watch your pet squeal in delight as it clambers over the millet, hulling each small seed as it goes. Millet, however, is also slightly goitrogenic and should never be used as the primary food source. The key is moderation and variety.

Supplements

If your parakeet is eating a well-rounded variety that includes plenty of fresh foods and a formulated base diet, it probably does not require any supplements at all. If it is a fussy eater that consumes mostly seed, however, it is likely deficient in several key vitamins and minerals. While you work to move it to a healthier diet, discuss appropriate supplementation with your veterinarian. There are dozens of different bird vitamins on the market that are designed to be added to the water or sprinkled on fresh foods, but I dislike adding supplements to the water for several reasons.

First of all, heavier but critical minerals such as calcium usually precipitate out and sit uselessly at the bottom of the water dish. Secondly, most (but not all) vitamin manufacturers use a sugar base, often dextrose, to improve palatability and help keep the vitamins suspended in the water. The sugar base creates a superb medium for growing bacteria and can turn your pet's water dish into a dangerous bacterial soup over the course of the day. Vitamins in water also lose potency quickly. Finally, parakeets don't typically drink a lot of water and might not get a sufficient dose. You're much safer sprinkling the supplement on any type of fruit or cooked food that the bird will eat, and keeping the water dish sparkling clean with fresh water.

Other supplements your veterinarian might suggest are iodine, which typically *is* safely added to the water, and calcium, often in the form of a cuttlebone or mineral block. Breeding hens and growing chicks have especially high calcium needs, but even single pets might need a little added to the diet if they're eating mostly seed. You might also hear about some

supplements on the market that your parakeet definitely does not need! For many years, bird keepers were convinced that cage birds, including parakeets, required grit in order to digest their food. This is a fallacy that has been disproved repeatedly by researchers and veterinarians, but the myth still persists.

Some birds, such as pigeons and doves, swallow seeds whole. In order to remove the tough seed husks, these species swallow fine particles of sand or gravel that lodge in their ventriculus (also known as the gizzard, or muscular stomach). These particles act as grinding stones to crush the seed and remove the husk, which passes undigested through the bird's digestive tract. Parrots and parakeets, however, do not ever swallow whole seeds. They use their hooked beaks and muscular tongues to remove the seed husks and crush the seeds before they swallow. Grit is not only unnecessary for hook-billed birds, but it can cause severe digestive upset if the bird ingests too much.

If all of this sounds complicated, it really isn't. Just think of your parakeet as part of the family, and feed it the healthy foods you'd offer to any other family member. And, if your family's diet is mostly processed fast foods, your new pet might provide the inspiration to head down a healthier path together. Enjoy!

THE DAILY ROUTINE

Your parakeet will appreciate some structure in its life, but you don't need to keep rigid schedules. A simple daily routine will help your parakeet understand and anticipate how its day will unfold.

Parakeets like routine. In a wild flock, everything is dictated by the movement of the sun and the weather patterns. Time to forage, time to sleep, time to breed. This predictability in life leaves them free to expend their energy on more important stuff, like avoiding predators, or maybe just having fun.

In captivity, your pet will be missing some of the external cues that guide its wild ancestors, but it will still appreciate some structure in its life. For example, when is breakfast served, and when is playtime? You don't have to set rigid schedules for every bit of interaction, but a simple daily routine will help your parakeet understand and anticipate how its day will unfold. It might also help you to remember what needs to be done each morning before you dash out the door and accidentally leave a hungry bird behind.

Most bird chores can be broken down into daily, weekly, and "as needed" categories. Daily chores will of course include feeding and playtime, while "as needed" chores will include

such variables as replacing worn perches and toys. It's a good idea to spend a few minutes writing down the tasks and going over them with family members, if applicable, before you even bring your bird home. Children especially can benefit from a checklist as they learn to handle the responsibility of pet care. If a child will be responsible for the bird's care and feeding, however, an adult should always supervise. And please, never let the parakeet go hungry in an effort to "teach" the children responsibility. The only thing that teaches is cruelty.

Daily Tasks

✔ Scrub and replace water dishes. The water must always be changed daily, even if it looks clean. Dangerous bacteria can be present, even without an obvious change in the water's appearance. In hot weather, or if the water is obviously fouled, you might need to replace it more than once per day. I like to keep multiple sets of dishes, and I run the dirty ones through the dishwasher to clean and sanitize them. Be aware that a quick rinsing might not remove germs thoroughly. Always scrub in hot soapy water, or put your dishwasher to work.

✔ Scrub and replace food dishes. Each morning, offer your parakeet a fresh dish of its base diet. Do not allow food to sit for days if it is uneaten. Pellets and seed can both become stale and rancid once exposed to air and light. Also, be aware that parakeets hull their seed before swallowing. What looks like a full seed dish to you is likely a dish filled with empty, discarded husks.

✔ Offer your bird a dish or hanging kebab of fresh chopped fruits and vegetables. You can either do this in the morning so that it has all day to explore (and hopefully eat) the goodies, or use these foods as a dinnertime treat.

Remember, fresh produce is an important part of a healthy parakeet's diet, so please don't forget this step. Always remove wet foods after a few hours (or as soon as you get home) because these are likely breeding grounds for bacteria and fungus.

✔ Sweep up any debris around the cage to prevent attracting insects or mice. You can change the cage bottom papers daily, or at least every few days. The longer you allow the cage to go between cleanings, the more likely you are to create odors and attract pests—and, the more likely you will be to place your parakeet's health at risk. Most diseases spread at least in part due to poor husbandry. Take this opportunity to look at your bird's droppings and take note of any changes that might signify health problems.

✔ Wipe down the cage area with a damp sponge. You do not need to use any fancy cleaners; in fact, some of them might be harmful to your bird. Just plain warm water works fine. If you need a little extra cleaning power, add a drop of dishwashing detergent or a few drops of white vinegar to the water. Both are healthy and bird-safe choices. There are also some products designed especially for use on bird cages. These are fine but might not work any better than the cheaper water and vinegar option.

✔ Always schedule some daily playtime! This can be an out-of-the-cage adventure or just a few minutes spent doing a good head scratch between the bars, but aim for some quality time every day. Your bird will survive if an illness or extra-long workday interferes occasionally, but please don't ignore your pet for days on end. We will talk more about playtime later in this chapter.

Weekly Tasks

✔ Remove all perches, toys, and dishes. Scrub perches and washable toys in hot soapy water and rinse well. Check toys for damage or frayed areas that could injure or trap the bird.

✔ Remove the cage tray and grate, and scrub both of them. Dry thoroughly before returning them to the cage.

✔ Wipe the cage bars inside and out with a damp sponge. Alternately, if a family member is available to play-sit, use this opportunity to let your parakeet out for some playtime while you do a heavy cleaning. Be sure the bird is properly supervised, and remove everything from the cage. Most parakeet cages are small enough to fit in a bathtub or shower, where you can take advantage of the running hot water to give the bars and base a good scrubbing and rinse. Dry carefully with a soft cloth, and replace perches, toys, and—of course—food and water dishes before you return the bird.

✔ Sweep or vacuum the area around the cage, and mop any hard surfaces.

✔ Rotate toys or add new ones to keep your parakeet entertained and busy. Replace cuttlebones or mineral blocks as needed.

As Needed Chores

✔ Periodically examine the parakeet's cage to check for cracks or warping in plastic parts, broken bar welds, or chipped paint. Replace or repair as needed.

✔ Replace perches that are badly chewed or cracked. Bacteria and parasites can live in those cracks if given the chance.

✔ If your bird has been ill, or if it has been in contact with other sick birds or animals, consider disinfecting the cage. To disinfect, first remove the parakeet to a safe and supervised place away from where you will be doing the cleaning. Remove all items such as dishes, perches, and toys, and disinfect if possible or replace. Clean the cage thoroughly in hot soapy water, and let it dry. You can purchase a suitable disinfectant from your veterinarian, or use a 1:10 solution of household chlorine bleach and water. To make a 1:10 solution, you need one part bleach for every nine parts water. For example, add ¼ cup (59 ml) bleach to 2¼ cups (532 ml) warm water and mix in a clean spray bottle. Never add any other ingredients because toxic fumes can form. Spray the mixture generously onto every inch of the cage, and let it sit for ten minutes. (It's best to do this in a tub or laundry sink so that other surfaces aren't damaged by the bleach.) After ten minutes, rinse carefully and dry completely. Always do this in a well-ventilated area, because bleach fumes are very harsh. And, of course, keep your bird safely in another room so that the caustic fumes don't damage its delicate respiratory tract. Don't ever use any disinfectant that isn't approved for use around birds. If you are uncertain, call your veterinarian for advice.

Bathing and Grooming

Okay, your parakeet's cage is spotless, but what about the bird? Healthy keets usually spend a great deal of time and care meticulously grooming their feathers. They will definitely appreciate the opportunity for an occasional bath. You can purchase bird baths that clip onto the cage door, or use a flat, shallow bowl that you can place on the cage floor. Fill it about ½ inch (1.3 cm) deep with

the grooming. Budgies are small enough to control with one hand as you use your other hand to wield the clippers, but you will have an easier time with an assistant, at least until you become more comfortable with the task. Ask your veterinarian or the bird's seller to demonstrate the process for you once so that you understand the correct technique. It's very important to avoid placing pressure on the parakeet's chest during restraint; birds cannot move air in and out of their body if their chest is compressed and will suffocate if held too tightly.

For nail trims, look closely at the curvature of each nail. The blood supply or "quick" should be visible as a red or dark line inside the clear nail. If you cut into this, it is painful for your bird and the nail will bleed, sometimes copiously. Just clip a little bit off the end of each

lukewarm water, and give your bird some privacy to bathe.

At first, it might be hesitant and refuse. After about an hour, remove the bowl or bath, and simply try it again in a few days. Eventually, your pet should be happy to jump in and splash around. Another option is to use a spray bottle filled with warm water, and mist the bird gently. Some birds love this and will dance and flap while you spray them. Others are more fearful and might not enjoy the process. Don't force it on your parakeet if it does not seem to like the water, or it might think it is being punished. Bath time should be fun.

Although parakeets do a great job of grooming themselves, you will have to take over when it comes to nail and wing trims. You will need the proper tools: a pair of sharp but blunt-tipped scissors, a pair of bird (or cat) claw clippers, and a tube of styptic powder in case of accidental bleeding. You can use flour or cornstarch instead, but styptic powder works much better and is easily available in any pet store. You should also have an assistant who can gently restrain the bird while you do

nail, staying far away from the blood vessel. If you accidentally cut too short and the nail bleeds, place a pinch of styptic powder (or flour) onto your fingertip, and hold it against the bleeding nail with gentle pressure until the bleeding stops. You should not have to trim the nails too often, just when you notice them curving sharply or causing your keet difficulty as it walks or climbs.

Wing trims (also called wing clips) are a little more important and should be performed with care. The idea of a wing trim is to remove a portion of the long primary flight feathers in order to hamper flight. Wing clips are not painful and cause no permanent damage; they are the equivalent of a birdie haircut. The cut feathers molt out naturally over time and are replaced by new feathers. That's why wing clips need to be performed regularly. Some people

are highly opposed to wing trimming and believe strongly that pet birds should remain fully flighted. Of course, wild birds need flight to survive, but flight can actually be deadly to our companion birds. A startled parakeet that is fully flighted can attain a great deal of speed, only to slam into a wall, window, or ceiling fan with fatal results, or bolt out of an open door and be lost forever. This isn't an obscure possibility; I have seen it happen with depressing frequency to bird owners who believe their pet would never do such a thing. A properly clipped parakeet can still fly a bit, but it can't gain a lot of altitude or speed. It is much safer for the bird and much easier for the human who needs to quickly catch their pet and remove it from harm's way.

To perform a wing clip, gently restrain the bird and stretch its wing out carefully so that you can clearly see all of the feathers. If you cut too many feathers, the bird will temporarily have difficulty flying at all and might be subject to injuries from falls. If you don't cut enough, it will still be able to fly well. Beginning at the end of the wing, carefully cut off the first five to eight primary flight feathers at a spot right below the primary coverts (the shorter feathers that overlap the long flight feathers). Point the scissors away from the bird's body so that you don't accidentally poke it if it struggles, and cut each feather cleanly one at a time—don't hack or saw at the feather shafts. You can start with five feathers and increase it to eight if the parakeet still seems to fly strongly.

Most importantly, do not ever cut any feather that is still encased in its waxy sheath. These growing feathers are known as "blood feathers," and they will bleed heavily if cut or injured. It is sometimes hard to get damaged blood feathers to stop bleeding because they act as wicks from the blood supply, and it might be necessary to remove the feather from its follicle to stem the blood flow. If this happens, don't panic. Hold the bird's wing firmly at a spot nearest the bleeding feather, and use a pair of strong tweezers or needle-nosed pliers to grasp the feather as close to the skin as possible. Quickly and smoothly pull out the feather in the direction of growth. This does hurt, and your keet will probably protest loudly, but it is necessary to prevent dangerous blood loss. With gentle pressure, hold some styptic powder or flour against the follicle for a minute until the bleeding stops.

Playtime

As mentioned earlier, playtime is a non-negotiable part of your bird's welfare. If you have multiple budgies housed together that are not hand-tamed and prefer to stay in the safety of their cage, be sure they have a roomy environment and plenty of stimulating toys. Even untamed birds might enjoy some playtime with humans, whether it's talking, singing, or just laughing at their antics.

If you have tame parakeets, you should use playtime as an opportunity to strengthen your bond. There are numerous freestanding playpens for parakeets that will fit onto your desk or a counter. Parakeets typically love swings and climbing gyms, but friendly birds might just want to use your body as a playpen! Once

you get to know your pet, you will learn what games it enjoys the most. Some keets enjoy verbal games, such as whistling or imitating sounds. Other parakeets enjoy chase or fetch games, and a few will retrieve a toy that the owner tosses, just like a dog. Sometimes the game is reversed, and the owner is supposed to repeatedly pick up an item that the bird tosses.

Don't think that toys need to be complicated and bird-specific. Some favorite items are small Dixie cups, which are great for hide-and-seek with treats; plastic Wiffle balls for fetch; card-

Simon Says

One of my parakeets plays a game that begins with him whistling a short series of notes. My job is to repeat the sequence back to him. At each turn he increases the speed, complexity, or number of notes, until I invariably fail to get the correct pattern. Then we begin again. He always wins!

board tissue boxes to create birdie forts; and clean, unused Popsicle sticks for chewing. You can also create a playtime necklace for yourself

by stringing colorful plastic beads, untreated wooden shapes, and small bells onto a leather or plastic cord. Tie various items at intervals, place it around your neck, and let your budgie explore these items instead of your expensive, real jewelry. You won't win any fashion awards, but you are likely to win your parakeet's heart! Just use common sense and don't let your keet chew on anything that is dirty, moldy, or possibly toxic.

Birdie Bedtime

After a hard day of playing and eating, your pet requires a good night's sleep. In general, parakeets should have about ten hours per night of uninterrupted sleep, plus periodic daytime naps. The best way to ensure sweet dreams is to invest in a cover for your bird's cage. It doesn't have to be fancy or custom-made. Any piece of plain, dark fabric will do. Avoid bright colors and patterns or highly textured fabrics that might catch a toenail and entangle the bird. For this reason, I don't like towels. Just be sure the cover is sturdy, washable, and heavy enough to stay put without sliding off every time a slight breeze hits.

When you first begin covering the cage, your pet might be frightened. Speak gently and move slowly, telling the bird in a happy voice that it's bedtime. It will soon learn to welcome and appreciate the cover. If possible, dim or turn off the lights in the room. If your parakeet is in the same room with the family television, be considerate and keep the sound down. You don't have to speak in whispers or forgo your evening of *Desperate Housewives*, but reduce gratuitous noise as much as possible. Parakeets are adaptable and will learn to

live with whatever is normal for your household, but maybe you need to take a cue from your pet and get a good night's sleep as well!

Of course, don't forget to uncover the bird in a timely manner in the morning. Your keet will be very unhappy if it hears its "flock" moving about and talking while it is still sitting in the dark. To a flock animal, this would feel like abandonment and shunning of the worst order. Greet the bird in a cheerful voice as you approach the cage, and gently remove the cover. Time to start the day!

It's All Fun and Games

Although toys and play are an integral part of your parakeet's life, it doesn't need to be complicated or pricey. You can make toys and play stands yourself with some common household items and a dash of creativity. Just use common sense, and keep safety in mind. Don't use items that are potentially toxic if your keet chews on them, or that pose a danger of trapping or falling on the bird. Here are some ideas to get you started:

✔ For an inexpensive play stand, fill a large bucket or flower pot with clean play sand, which should be available at any home improvement store. Gather some forked branches from safe trees, scrub thoroughly in hot soapy water, and let dry. Stick the branches in the sand, and you have a play tree for your pet. What is a "safe tree?" Basically, any tree that is not listed as toxic (check online or ask your veterinarian) and that has not been exposed to pesticides, fungicides, excessive automobile exhaust, or other chemicals. I'm not including a list of safe plants here, because it could fill an entire book, and the evidence is often confusing and contradictory. For example, some trees have poisonous leaves, but the bark is safe (or vice versa). Others may be poisonous to cattle, but not birds, and so on. Your county's Cooperative Extension Office can also give you guidelines about what's safe. The biggest danger is diseases or parasites from wild birds, so scrub those branches carefully! If they will fit, you can also bake the branches in the oven at a low temperature—about 200°F (93°C)—for an hour to kill any beasties that might be lurking under the bark.

✔ Another inexpensive play stand is a wooden drying rack for clothes. These folding racks are available in just about any home goods store, and are usually reasonably priced. Because they fold away when not in use, they're a great choice for people with limited space. Your pet can perch on the various dowels, and there's lots of room to hang toys. They are large enough to allow plenty of exercise, and easy to clean. Just be aware that they tip easily, so place the stand where it won't get bumped.

✔ Many children's toys make great toys for parakeets. Small plastic cars and trucks can be fun for an active keet to push around. Some birds enjoy riding on top of larger toy cars, provided the "driver" doesn't push the car too quickly. Small stuffed animals are fun to preen, and your budgie might love to roll and chase marbles or small balls. I have a colorful bead maze designed for human toddlers that absolutely fascinates my birds. They love to slide and twirl the beads, and it keeps them quiet for long stretches of time. Children's toys are non-toxic, but be aware of any small pieces that the bird might break off and inadvertently swallow.

✔ Some cat toys are (ironically) great parakeet toys. Small plastic balls and rolling barrels with jingle bells inside are super inexpensive and common among cat supplies. Your keet might also enjoy chasing the "toy on a stick" cat teasers that incorporate a small fuzzy toy on an elastic cord attached to a stick. Simply drag the toy slowly past your pet, and see if a chase ensues. One word of caution: always supervise carefully when allowing your bird to play with a jingle bell. The design of these bells incorporates small cut-outs that can trap a curious beak. I never allow larger parrots to play with jingle bells, because they have a tendency to bite down and crush the bell onto their beak tip. I have had to remove such crushed bells from parrot faces, and it is not a pleasant experience. Budgies, however, don't typically have the beak strength to do such damage, and they really enjoy tossing these bells about. Just don't tempt fate and leave the bells in the cage when you're not around to keep an eye on them.

✔ Certain common household products have surprisingly good toy potential. At Loro Parque, the world-renowned parrot park in Tenerife, Canary Islands, the trainers use plastic drinking straws as a reward for the performing parrots. They are chewy, non-toxic, and probably resemble the texture of feather sheaths, which might promote healthy preening. Most parrots love to chew on these, and it's an extra bonus if you get the fast-food restaurant ones wrapped in paper that the bird can peel off first. If drinking straws are too big and clumsy for your keet, plastic coffee stirrers work just fine. Small paper cups can be used to hide treats, and make a satisfying echo chamber for chattering budgies when they stick their heads inside. Brand new toothbrushes or other household brushes are great preening toys. Of course, do not ever let your pet play with used brushes that can harbor germs or toxins. Actually, just plain old white paper crumpled into a ball can keep your bird busy pushing, tearing, and chewing it to bits. Just use your imagination, but keep safety in mind as well.

Most importantly, make sure your parakeet is having fun. There's sometimes a fine line between play and inadvertent bullying. It might seem funny to you if your pet is startled by a new toy and scrambles frantically to escape, but it's sure not funny to the keet. It will probably forgive you for accidentally

frightening it once or twice, but repetitive scares will teach the bird that you can't be trusted. Always introduce novel items in a slow and patient manner, and take your lead from how the bird reacts. As your pet gains confidence in its environment and learns to trust, it will become more adventurous and open to new playthings.

UNDERSTANDING YOUR PARAKEET

When you bring a young keet home, it will desire the same interaction and sense of belonging that it would have in nature. Therefore, you and your family will become its surrogate flock, so be sure to spend lots of time interacting with this social bird.

Humans are predators. We stalk through our lives believing that our brains set us apart from the rest of the animal kingdom, and we usually don't fear much, except perhaps death and taxes. And, all too often we lack the empathy to see the world through the eyes of our animal companions. It is this lack of awareness that causes the most frequent misunderstandings between pets and people, especially between pet birds and their human "flock mates."

Birds, you must remember, are prey animals. Their entire existence is predicated on being the least visible, or the fastest, or—if all else fails—the most intimidating member of a group. The most conspicuous, the slowest, and the apparent weakest are quickly picked off by predators. That's why mutations don't often survive for long in the wild. Would you want to be the only blue parakeet in a sea of green when a hawk is circling? Not only is that bird at extreme risk, but its mate and offspring run a higher than normal risk by being near such a target. If that doesn't put a damper on romance and reduce a bird's chances of finding a mate and passing on its genes, nothing will.

The Life of a Prey Animal

It's hard work to stay alive in the wild when there are hungry predators everywhere that are trying to catch you. It requires tremendous vigilance and well-honed senses. Luckily, nature did supply your parakeet with some tools and skills to protect it. Consider these factors:

✔ The wing of a parakeet is designed for agility and maneuverability. It can fly at a top speed of 36 miles per hour (58 km/h) and take off quickly, but that speed pales in comparison to its likely predators. For example, the Peregrine Falcon is the fastest animal on earth, able to reach a top speed of over 200 miles per hour (322 km/h) during its hunting stoop. The parakeet, however, can use its agility to turn and twirl and outmaneuver a falcon in many situations.

✔ A parakeet's wild feather coloration of mostly green and black is an effective camouflage against the scrubby grasslands in which it lives. An individual budgie standing still among the vegetation would be nearly invisible. And, in a flock situation, the colors and patterns blend in a manner that makes it difficult for a predator to zero in on individuals.

✔ Your parakeet's eyes are the eyes of a prey species. Predators typically have eyes that are set close together and face forward so that they can focus with intense binocular vision when tracking prey. For example, hawks have an overlapping field of view of 30 to 50 degrees for binocular vision, and an overall field of view of about 150 degrees. Prey species, on the other hand, have eyes that are set widely apart, usually on the sides of their heads. Forward (binocular) vision isn't as important as is the ability to detect the movement of a potential predator sneaking up out of the brush. Therefore, pigeons—a popular lunch entrée for many raptors—have a binocular area that is only about 20 to 30 degrees, but a total field of vision of 300 to 340 degrees. Nature made it really hard

to sneak up on pigeons in order to give them a fighting chance at survival.

The Flock Mentality

Living in a flock offers many benefits for parakeets. Animals that live cooperatively in flocks or colonies enjoy most of the same perks that drive humans to form societies. Think of a single budgie in the wild: it would have to find food, shelter, and companionship on its own. It wouldn't sleep well because it would never know when that predator was going to show up. It would not be able to fulfill the basic driving instinct to pass on its genes, unless it found another single bird that happened to be of the opposite sex and didn't already have a mate. Although budgies aren't as strongly monogamous as some other parrot species, they do tend to keep the same mate for life, albeit with an occasional fling on the side.

In a flock, however, all of the above problems are greatly mitigated. Instead of a single bird flying in search of food, there are hundreds—often thousands—of pairs of eyes scouting for a patch of seeding grasses or an inviting waterhole. When a member of the group spots food or water, it loudly broadcasts its discovery to the rest. The flock then converges to feast. While most of the individuals are eating and drinking, some sentinels always remain on alert, scanning the surrounding area for a glimpse of potential predators. If one is spotted, the watchers sound the alarm to send

the other birds scurrying for safety. At night, a communal roost serves much the same purpose. Although a stealthy snake or owl might be able to sneak up on a single parakeet, it's a lot more difficult to sneak up on a large colony without being noticed.

Parakeets, in fact, spend their whole lives in cooperative groups. Due to the uncertain nature of their food and water supply, they lead a rather nomadic existence, but they never travel alone. The flock moves across the land until they find a suitable place to temporarily settle and reproduce. Usually, the mated pairs nest in close proximity, and it's not uncommon to see adults helping to tend their neighbors' chicks. This supportive environment not only

helps the youngsters to survive; it also gives the parents a little more freedom to forage and maintain their own strength. The flocks have a well-defined "language" that allows the members to communicate easily, and the birds spend a lot of time in social activities such as mutual preening and play.

The Pet Parakeet

With all this in mind, it should be easy to understand that a highly social creature like a parakeet needs companionship and structure in its life, just as surely as it needs other types of sustenance. When you bring a young parakeet into your home, you and other family members

won't understand that it is safe from the owl in its cage indoors. So many things that we take for granted might be very frightening to a pet bird. Try to be empathetic to potential fears, and either remove the threat or work to gently show the budgie that it is safe and protected.

Bonding and Imprinting

Bonding and imprinting are two words that are thrown around quite a bit in relation to taming birds, and they are often quite misunderstood. "Filial" imprinting occurs most frequently in ducks, geese, and other precocial chicks whose survival depends on their ability to follow their mother shortly after hatching. These chicks focus on the first suitable "mother" substitute they see during a critical period after hatching, believed to be about thirteen to sixteen hours post-hatch. The process occurs much later in species such as raptors, which usually imprint between two and five weeks of age. Filial imprinting has led to many feel-good movies, such as *Fly Away Home,* in which an ultra-light aircraft enthusiast taught orphaned Canadian geese how to migrate after he raised them and they imprinted to him. Birds that imprint very strongly to humans sometimes can't be released back into the wild because they have no interest in their own species and look to humans for food and companionship. Their self-identity tells them they *are* humans.

There is, however, a current scientific debate on whether imprinting is reversible. Some scientists claim that imprinted birds can and do learn to revise their self-image. In one account of an orphaned tawny owl, the bird was found abandoned as a very young chick.

and pets become the keet's surrogate flock. It will yearn for the same interaction and sense of belonging that it would have in nature. This is a largely instinctual desire and won't be decreased simply because the chick was born in captivity. If it is kept alone in a cage far from family activity, it will feel ostracized from its human flock and might become depressed or fearful. As I've said before in this book, do not bring home a pet parakeet unless you are willing to integrate it into your daily life.

In addition, your parakeet will always view the world just a little differently than you will. That whirling ceiling fan that you use to cool the house might look an awful lot like the wings of an onrushing hawk. The pet cat that strolls past the cage is a skilled predator. (Of course, some budgies and cats become great friends, but they should always be closely monitored.) Your keet might enjoy watching wild finches and sparrows at a bird feeder outside a nearby window, but if an owl appears, the keet will feel just as terrified as the outside birds. It

He was named Eric by his rescuers, and lived as a tame pet in captivity for seven years. One day Eric escaped, and he returned to visit his owner a few weeks later with a mate at his side. The crafty owl had managed to figure out hunting and other survival skills, and had even attracted a mate, after living his entire life with humans. Eric also apparently maintained his fondness for his human friend, as he would frequently pop by for a quick visit.

Bonding is a term that is often used interchangeably with imprinting, but it is really quite different. Parakeets (and numerous other bird species) are known as "pair-bonders," which means they form very close relationships with a mate and usually remain together for life. They will re-mate in the event of their original mate's death, or in rare cases of incompatibility and "birdie divorce." When pair-bonding birds are kept in captivity, their natural instincts will push them to form a similar close bond with a human. They are not suffering from any sort of identity confusion like an imprinted bird, but they are willing to overlook the species difference in order to create a relationship. This is the typical loving rapport that occurs between a companion parakeet and a devoted owner.

Don't let anyone try to convince you that you must purchase a very young or even unweaned chick in order for it to bond to you. They are confusing imprinting and bonding, and imprinting is not something you want to attain. A parakeet of any age can bond with its owner, provided it gets plenty of love and attention.

Taming and Training Your Parakeet

If you purchase a young parakeet that is well socialized to humans, you will probably not have to worry about taming—you will just need to make friends with an already tame bird. If the bird is older or not used to handling, it might require a bit of taming before it accepts handling. In either case, the process is the same. An older bird might just take a little longer to respond.

When you first bring your pet home, do not immediately attempt to handle it. Give it a few days to get used to its new surroundings. Always approach the cage slowly while talking in a quiet and soothing voice. Be careful not to startle the keet by suddenly popping through a doorway next to the cage. I always announce my movements to new birds by talking or whistling as I move through the house. Tell children to use quiet voices and avoid running or screeching near the cage. You won't have to tiptoe around forever—once the bird gets used to you and its new home, it will become much calmer and able to tolerate normal household chaos.

When the parakeet becomes more comfortable, it will begin to explore its cage and play with toys. At this point, you can begin to make friends. A few times a day, offer a special treat like a piece of spray millet through the cage bars. As soon as it is accepting the treat from your fingers, you can progress to placing your hand with the treat inside the cage. Do not chase the bird around or push the treat at its face; just hold your hand as still as possible until the keet approaches you. An already tame bird might hop onto your finger after a day or

so, but a very timid parakeet might take weeks to respond. The key is patience and repetition. Do not panic and jerk back if the bird jabs at you with its beak. It is testing you to see what happens. If you immediately pull back, it will either develop a fear of hands or decide that it can bully you. Neither scenario bodes well for your future relationship.

Even if it actively bites your hand, try to ignore it and hold steady. Parakeet bites pinch and are unpleasant, but they don't have the beak strength to do any real harm. Say "No!" firmly, and feel free to frown in an exaggerated manner. Pet birds are extremely visual creatures, and they are often quite skilled at reading human expressions. Your frown will tell them that biting is unacceptable, but they will appreciate the fact that you didn't react aggressively or in anger. Again, this is a test;

stay calm and patient, and you will pass with flying colors!

Once the bird is comfortable on your finger, you can try to pet it. Most parakeets love to be scratched on their head, neck, and face. Birds are individuals, and you might find that your bird hates having its feet touched, or loves having its back rubbed, or whatever. Let its reaction guide you to what it likes. A tame parakeet will likely want to return the favor by preening your hair and clothing. Mutual preening is an extremely important facet of social bonding in the parakeet world. You should be quite honored that you have been chosen for the task.

Speech Training

Teaching a parakeet to talk is pretty easy: just talk to your bird! In general, birds are most likely to imitate voices that are higher in pitch and words that are spoken with a lot of emotion. (That's why parrot species often learn to curse like sailors.) To facilitate the process, choose a word or phrase you'd like the budgie to learn, and repeat it often in a friendly and emphatic manner. Don't be discouraged if nothing seems to happen for a very long time. In my experience, parrots seem to process speech in their heads for a long period of time before they make an attempt to actually say their first words. Eventually, your pet will begin to sound out the words. At first, it might be garbled or unclear, but the keet will continue to practice with your encouragement. Once it learns a little speech and gains confidence that you recognize what it is saying, subsequent words will come much faster. You might hear it rehearsing at night after its cage is covered. For some reason, many birds love to mumble themselves to sleep with speech practice.

You can also purchase any number of CDs or DVDs that promise to teach your bird to talk. The idea is that you leave these playing during the day when you're not home, and your pet will soon learn to recite the complete works of Shakespeare. (Well, not quite, but you get the idea.) Truthfully, I'm not a big fan of these programs. They might work, but I want my keets to learn to speak through their interaction with me as part of bonding and playtime. Brainwashing them with an endless loop of canned words isn't nearly as effective or fun. And be cautious about teaching your budgie to whistle a tune. Although they are quite

talented whistlers, I have found that some birds are less inclined to talk after they have learned to whistle. If you want a talking bird, teach them words first, and you can experiment with whistling later.

Above all, learn to relax and enjoy your pet. As I've said repeatedly, all parakeets (and people) are individuals. Your personal relationship with a pet parakeet won't be the same as your friend's or neighbor's or even another family member's relationship with the keet. The unique bond you form can give you a lifetime of love and laughter, depending only on how much time and love you are willing to invest.

Trick Training

There's a common misconception that budgies are not as intelligent as their larger parrot cousins, and that they don't make suitable candidates for trick training. Nothing could be further from the truth! Budgies are smart and eminently trainable, but they do have some factors working against them: they tend to be hyperactive and distractible, and they usually have a short attention span. This makes training a little more challenging, but mostly it requires just a dab of extra patience from the trainer.

Before you consider any type of advanced training, you must first win your bird's absolute trust. It must jump onto your finger readily when offered, and not flutter off in a panic when you move. Do not attempt to push the keet into learning tricks until it is relaxed and attentive on your hand. To begin, you must first teach the "step up" command. This is an absolutely essential basic method to control the bird and retrieve it quickly from potential danger if it gets away from you, much the same as the "come" command for dogs. "Step up" is simply the formal command to tell the keet to step onto your finger. Even if your bird is already doing this regularly, it's still important that it understands the verbal cue. To execute, gently press your finger against the keet's lower abdomen, while saying "step up." Don't place your finger so high on the bird's chest that it has to use its beak to pull up, or so low against its legs that it is trapped against the perch; it should be a comfortable and easy step from the perch to your finger.

As soon as the keet steps onto your finger, praise it lavishly while repeating the command: *"Good step up! Good bird!"* The goal here is to ingrain the command so deeply into your pet that it responds immediately each time. You can turn this practice into a game by playing "ladder" with the bird. To play, command *"Step up,"* praise the bird, and immediately repeat the command using the finger from your other hand. With this method, you are simulating a ladder climb. It's a great training drill, and good exercise to boot. Not only that, but most birds enjoy the game. Of course, quit as soon as the bird loses interest or appears tired, or it will seem more like drudgery than fun. Keep all training sessions to no more than 15 minutes, or less if your pet seems stressed or bored. Training should always be fun!

Once your pet has mastered the fine art of stepping up, you can move on to more challenging tricks. There are several different methods of training, but I like target training for budgies. The target method was originally designed for training marine mammals, and is brilliant in its simplicity. The animal is consistently rewarded for touching or positioning itself near a specific object. By manipulating the "target," the trainer can teach the animal to spin, twirl, jump through hoops, or perform many other tricks.

To begin target training, get a small supply of your keet's absolute favorite treat—millet spray usually works well, or a piece of one of those sticky seed bells—and a colorful, easily recognizable chopstick or other small stick. Hold the chopstick outside of the cage but in view of the bird, and gradually move it closer as your pet becomes comfortable with the sight of it. Be aware this might take several sessions or more until the bird decides that the object is not scary. Once it is unafraid and appears curious, slowly move the chopstick near the bars where the bird can touch it. Do not poke at the keet or force the chopstick toward it, but hold it so that the bird can approach and touch it with its beak. Again, it might take several sessions, but as soon as your keet touches it, immediately praise *"Good target! Good bird!"* and quickly offer a treat. Keep practicing and reinforcing until the bird races over to touch the target every time it sees it. The process does take patience, but once the target concept is firmly established, other tricks can follow quickly.

I have to interject here that I don't usually like to use food rewards for training birds, because I train a lot of larger parrots that quickly grasp the quid pro quo: no treat, no tricks. They will sometimes refuse to blink until they see solid proof that a food reward is pending. For hyper little budgies, however, nothing seems to focus their attention better than a tasty morsel of spray millet. You might find that your pet works better for praise alone, or for a head scratch, or whatever. Feel free to adapt these methods to best fit your unique relationship with your pet.

Once your keet is targeting like a champ, you can use the target to create tricks. For example, you can use cardboard toilet paper rolls or short lengths of PVC pipe to teach your bird to *"Tunnel."* Place the keet at one end of the tube, command "tunnel," and wave the target at the other end. The parakeet will most likely scramble through the tunnel to reach its target. After several repetitions (and treats and praise) the bird will respond to the "tunnel" command even if the target isn't there. You can adapt the same method to get it to climb a wooden ladder, shinny up a rope, jump through a hoop, or spin in circles. Just

give each trick a unique command, and gradually remove the target when the bird learns to perform the trick effortlessly.

This is just a brief overview of some simple training tips. Just remember to keep it fun, and always try to end sessions on a positive note. If you feel yourself getting frustrated because the bird isn't responding as you had hoped, end the training immediately for the day. Some actions might take a long time to learn, while others come quickly. And even if your parakeet turns out to be a birdie school dropout, the time you spend together will enrich both of your days.

Once you begin to pay close attention to your parakeet's body language, you'll soon be able to gain a keen understanding of your bird's emotions and moods. Remember, it will likely be watching you as well in an attempt to understand *your* emotions and moods. After a while, the two of you should come to a comfortable and mutual appreciation of each other's unspoken language. In the meantime, the following is a description of some of the more common postures and what they mean.

✔ Head down, head feathers ruffled, back of the neck exposed: this is a clear invitation for petting. Your parakeet is relaxed and is asking for a head scratch and a neck rub. This is a very vulnerable position and displays a great amount of trust.

✔ Head up, feathers on the head and neck ruffled, beak open, possibly leaning backward: the bird is frightened. Step back and speak softly to reassure it. It would assume this ruffled posture in the wild in an attempt to look bigger and more intimidating to a possible threat.

✔ Head up, standing tall, feathers tight against the body, motionless: this is also a fear response. When wild parakeets see a potential predator, their first response is to freeze in place and hope the predator passes by without spotting them. If they realize they have been sighted, their next response would be to fly wildly for cover. Back away from a bird in this position; if you continue toward it, it might thrash wildly and injure itself.

✔ Head up, cheek and head feathers possibly ruffled, eyes flashing or "pinning": the parakeet is excited. Keets and other parrots have the ability to constrict and dilate the pupils of their eyes in response to various stimuli. When your pet is pacing back and forth, and its pupils are just tiny black dots in the middle of its irises, it is showing you that it is very excited about something. Of course, excitement can be good or bad. It might be extremely happy to see you and knows that it will be let out of its cage to play soon, or it might be furious that the cat just ran past its cage and startled it. Always try to look at this posture in context with whatever else is going on in the bird's environment.

✔ Upright but slouched posture, body and/or head feathers slightly ruffled, cheek feathers ruffled, possibly perching on one foot: this is a relaxed and probably sleepy parakeet. Unlike other parrots, healthy budgies do sometimes sleep while perching on two legs. It might also bury its face into its back feathers or under a wing for a serious nap. See below, and note that this can also be a sign of illness if the bird is lethargic, slow to rouse, or shows other symptoms.

✔ Ruffled feathers, glassy eyes, lethargic, slouched on the perch on both feet: this bird is likely ill, possibly very ill. See the chapter on Buying a Companion Parakeet for additional signs of illness. Sometimes sleepy and sick look a lot alike, but a sleepy parakeet snaps to attention when something catches its interest; a sick bird won't look quite right, even if it tries to look normal.

✔ Ruffled head feathers, head tilted to one side, parakeet softly chirping: the bird is flirting with you. Now might be a good time for some cuddling and head-scratching.

✔ Crouched down, body quivering, wings held slightly away from body, head possibly thrown back with beak open: the meaning of this posture depends on the age and sex of the bird. This is the posture of a baby bird begging for food. This can also be the posture of a sexually mature female that is soliciting a male, or what she considers to be a suitable human replacement.

✔ Wiping its beak vigorously against a perch or other object: in most cases, this is done simply to clean and polish the beak after eating, or to remove annoying keratin flakes. In some cases, it can be a sign of frustration or displaced anger. Usually, however, it is just simple grooming.

✔ Fluffing out all of its feathers and shaking vigorously, sometimes wagging its tail back and forth for a moment: this is usually a transition between activities, a way of saying "okay, what's next?" It feels good and helps remove dust and debris from the feathers.

✔ Suddenly stopping what it is doing and taking a few steps backward: poop alert! Even tiny young chicks in the nest will usually back up a bit before defecating in order to keep the nest somewhat clean. The bird might also wiggle or lift its tail just before it passes the dropping.

✔ Beak grinding: this is something that parakeets do when they are very content and relaxed, usually just before falling asleep. You might hear a soft grinding sound coming from the cage after you cover your pet for the night.

✔ Regurgitating food: this is a parakeet's way of saying "I love you." Try not to be grossed out—it is quite a compliment. If you want it to stop, gently divert the bird's attention to something else and it will usually re-swallow the "gift" as it is distracted.

This is not a complete list of parakeet behaviors, but it will give you a start at interpreting what your bird is trying to tell you. Over time, it will all make sense, and you and your keet will be able to communicate easily in your own unique manner.

COMMON ILLNESSES AND HEALTH CARE

Make sure to get to know your pet so you are aware of any changes in behavior. If you notice an abnormal trend in behavior that doesn't resolve in a day or two, call your avian veterinarian.

When your human friends don't feel so good, they can tell you. In fact, they might be only too happy to regale you with tales of their symptoms and suspicions. It's a different story when your parakeet becomes ill. It will not be able to ask for your help or say what hurts; it will be completely dependent on you to be aware that something is not right and offer appropriate assistance.

Unfortunately, prey animals such as birds instinctively try to hide their symptoms, lest they attract a predator looking for an easy target. Keeping up with the flock is the only way to survive in the wild. Sick or injured birds are picked off quickly. By the time your keet is so sick that it is showing obvious signs, it is likely gravely ill and unable to maintain the façade of normalcy. How, then, will you know when something is wrong?

The trick is to know your pet, and be aware of subtle signs. If a normally boisterous budgie is sitting quietly on the perch for long stretches, it could be a sign. If an enthusiastic eater suddenly begins to shun food, it could be

a sign. Of course, parakeets—like people—can have an "off" day here or there, but if you notice an abnormal trend in behavior that doesn't resolve in a day or two, it's time to call your avian veterinarian.

Don't wait too long to seek help for a sick bird. Avian illnesses can progress very quickly, and any delay in treatment could mean death for your pet. When you call the veterinarian, be prepared to answer several basic questions. The veterinarian will want to know the bird's age, sex, and typical diet, as well as how long you've owned it, what symptoms are present, and how long it has been since you first noticed the symptoms. Don't be surprised if he or she also asks about other pets in the household, or about recent changes in the bird's environment. These are all questions that can help lead to an accurate diagnosis. In most cases, you will have to schedule an appointment to bring in your pet. If you feel the parakeet is critically ill, don't hesitate to explain that it's an emergency. However, don't ignore symptoms until it *becomes* an emergency.

An avian veterinarian once commented to me: "A broken wing is an emergency. A bird that has been allowed to decline from an infection for several days until the owner finally decided to do something about it is abuse."

One of the most important things you can do for emergency care is to supply heat. Parakeets have a very quick metabolism and a normal body temperature between 105° and 106°F (about 41°C), so a sick bird uses up a lot of strength just maintaining its body temperature. Until you can get your pet to a veterinarian, you can create a makeshift hospital cage by covering half the cage with a towel and placing a heating pad on top of the towel. You can also use a heat lamp near the cage, but be aware that these create more of a fire hazard—do not let it touch the towel or any other flammable material. Also be cautious and keep the cords from any electrical devices safely out of the bird's reach. Always leave a portion of the cage uncovered

so that the parakeet can move to a cooler spot if it becomes overheated. If your pet is having difficulty perching and is sitting on the floor of the cage, place water and food dishes on the floor nearby, but use shallow dishes. Deep water dishes might pose a drowning danger for a bird that is weak and disoriented. And, when traveling to the veterinarian, keep the cage covered, and preheat the car in cool weather. If your car has heated seats, consider using them to keep the cage or carrier warm.

At the Veterinarian's Office

Once you arrive at the clinic, keep your bird covered and safely away from other animals. It doesn't need to be stressed by staring at possible predators, and you don't want to endanger other pets if your parakeet has a communicable infection. Although dogs and

Signs of Illness

Avian illnesses can be subtle, but here are some common signs:

✔ Does the bird sit quietly with its feathers fluffed up? Healthy but sleepy birds will fluff their feathers and slouch down to take a nap, but they are easily awakened and quick to alert. When awakened, they might yawn and stretch their wings. A sick parakeet will often sit fluffed and hunched, appear lethargic, and be slow to respond.

✔ Does the bird breathe heavily at rest? Signs of breathing trouble include wheezing or clicking sounds, and "tail bobbing," which means that the bird's tail pumps slowly up and down with each breath. This is a clear indication of respiratory distress. Be aware, however, that a healthy budgie that has just flown a distance or perched after wrestling with a toy might breathe heavily for a minute or two.

✔ Is there a change in eating or drinking habits? Is the bird suddenly ravenous, or is it uninterested in previously favored foods? Does it drink more or less than normal? Again, a healthy pet's hunger or thirst might vary a bit according to activity, season, or mood, but a change that lasts for more than a few days is a red flag. For example, a noticeable increase in thirst could be a warning sign of diabetes, infection, or a kidney tumor.

✔ Do you notice signs of poor grooming or matted feathers? A sick bird is probably in no mood to preen. Fecal matter pasted near the bird's vent can indicate diarrhea or other problems, and sticky food around the face or head might mean vomiting. Please note that there is a difference between voluntary regurgitation to a favorite toy or person in an attempt to "feed" their love, versus involuntary vomiting from illness. Usually, regurgitation is controlled and rather neat, but vomiting is harsher and often leaves partially eaten food stuck to the bird's face.

✔ Is the bird limping or lame? Sometimes a limp can indicate relatively minor foot problems or an injured leg, but it can also be a sign of much more serious problems, such as a kidney tumor pressing on the nerves leading to the leg. Always have a limp evaluated by a veterinarian.

✔ Are the bird's nostrils or eyes crusted or runny? Are its eyes half-closed or glassy-looking? A healthy bird should have clear, bright eyes and clean nostrils. There is, however, one exception: females in breeding condition might have a crusty-looking brownish cere (the fleshy part above the beak that contains the nostrils). If the bird shows no other signs of illness and has no trouble breathing, it is probably a normal breeding-age hen.

cats are unlikely to pick up a disease from it, other birds could be at risk.

After examining your budgie, the veterinarian will likely ask your permission to run some tests. Very few diseases can be identified through a simple physical exam. For example, a common bacterial infection that would readily respond to antibiotics might present with the exact same symptoms as a deadly viral disease. Without a way of telling the two apart, your veterinarian will be simply guessing at the correct treatment. Nothing is more frustrating to a caring practitioner than watching pets die needlessly because the owner is unwilling to pay for proper diagnostics. If you are in a financial bind and really cannot afford to pay for the tests, be honest. Some veterinary practices will allow you to pay over time, or might be willing to offer reduced pricing for an owner that is truly in need. At the very least, the veterinarian can prioritize the testing to choose which method will have the best chance of revealing what's wrong. Below are some of the most common tests.

• Gram's stains are used to determine the type and number of bacterium or yeast present in an infection. The veterinarian will use a sterile cotton swab to collect a fluid sample, usually from your bird's vent (cloaca) or mouth. The sample is smeared onto a microscope slide and treated with special dyes. Different types of bacteria absorb the dye in different manners and change colors, allowing them to be identified under a microscope. This test will tell the veterinarian if bacteria are the likely culprit and give a rough idea of which types are

present. Unfortunately, bacterial and yeast infections can occur secondary to other diseases, so this test does not rule out the presence of an underlying or more severe problem.

• Culture and sensitivity tests are often used in addition to Gram's stains, especially in cases of chronic infection. The veterinarian will use a fluid sample like the one above, except this time the sample is streaked across a culture plate filled with a special growth medium. The culture is placed into an incubator for a period of 24 to 48 hours. If there is significant bacterial or fungal growth, the laboratory technician can place small paper disks that are treated with various antibiotics onto the culture, in order to see which drug does the best job of killing the pathogen. Because some bacteria are resistant to many antibiotics, this test allows the veterinarian to prescribe the most effective medicine for the illness. Since cultures take a few days to process, your veterinarian might prescribe a broad-spectrum antibiotic immediately, and then fine-tune the medication after the culture results come back.

• A complete blood count (CBC) uses a small drop of the bird's blood, usually from a clipped toenail, to determine some measures of health. This test helps define levels of oxygen-rich red blood cells, infection-fighting white blood cells, clotting ability, and other blood components.

• A blood chemistry panel is a more complete type of blood test that indicates all sorts of metabolic and organic problems. It requires a little more blood, so the veterinarian will likely draw a bit from a vein in the parakeet's leg, neck, or wing. A "chem panel" will provide a great deal of information about the bird's overall health, organ function, and nutritional status.

- Fecal smears are used to detect intestinal parasites. The veterinarian will take a fresh dropping and examine it under a microscope to check for parasites. The sample must be very fresh, and not all samples will show signs of an infection, even if one is present. Some parasites, such as *Giardia,* can be difficult to detect.
- DNA probes are used to test for certain viral and bacterial infections, such as chlamydiosis, polyomavirus, and mycoplasma. These are highly specialized tests that are designed to find or rule out a specific disease. DNA tests can also be used to determine a bird's sex in species that are monomorphic (both sexes look identical).
- Radiographs, MRIs, and CT scans are used on birds, just like they are on people, to diagnose skeletal injuries and look for tumors. If your veterinarian discovers a tumor on the bird, he or she might recommend a biopsy to determine if the tumor is cancerous.

Home Care

After your parakeet is sent home, be sure to follow the veterinarian's instructions exactly. If you are nervous or unsure about administering medication, tell your veterinarian in advance and ask if the drug is available in another form. For example, if you are too squeamish to give an injection, perhaps it is possible to offer the drug orally. Many oral drugs can now be flavored, which makes them much more palatable. However, *never* give a drug in a manner or dosage that the veterinarian didn't approve. Doing so could kill or sicken your pet. Don't be embarrassed to admit you're afraid—the doctor or staff will likely be happy to spend some extra time with you offering instruction and tips on medicating the bird. Also, never stop a drug without the veterinarian's approval. Even if your pet seems miraculously better, the underlying disease might still be lying dormant, waiting to strike again. Follow the treatment schedule, no matter how healthy the parakeet seems. Of course, if the bird seems to be getting worse or develops additional symptoms, call the veterinarian immediately.

Although hygiene is always important, be extra vigilant when caring for a sick pet. Wash and dry your hands thoroughly before and after handling the bird. Although rare, some diseases can transmit from animal to animal, and some can even infect people. Those that pass from animals (or birds) to humans are called "zoonotic" diseases, and there are a few that parakeets can carry. These will be discussed later in this chapter. On the flip side, you can also transmit germs to your keet, including some nasty bacteria such as *E. coli* and the mycobacteria that cause tuberculosis. Never allow your parakeet to take food from your mouth, and avoid kissing it directly on the beak. And, of course, use common sense if you have other pet birds in the home. Quarantine the sick bird as discussed in the chapter on Bringing Home Your Pet, and discuss the possibility of contagion with your veterinarian.

Common Diseases

A healthy diet and good care will go a long way toward keeping your parakeet in top shape, but sometimes diseases strike in spite of our best efforts. A comprehensive list of pet bird diseases could fill several books this size, but there are some that are more common among companion parakeets. You might notice that the symptoms for many of the different diseases are nearly identical. That's why a trip to the veterinarian for proper testing is really the only way to determine what's going on. Otherwise, you will be playing a dangerous game of roulette with your keet's life.

Malnutrition

Sometimes people assume that a well-fed bird can't suffer from malnutrition, but that's far from true. What matters is *what* your bird eats, not necessarily how much food it consumes. In fact, one of the common indicators of malnutrition is obesity. Budgies are especially prone to obesity from a poor diet, and the high blood fat levels can cause heart disease, fatty tumors (lipomas), and liver degeneration.

Often, one of the first signs of liver damage is overgrown beaks and nails. A healthy keet should never require beak trimming, and just occasional nail trims. If your bird's beak looks longer than normal, or if it is flaky and chipped, it's possibly a sign of fatty liver disease. In its early stages, this disease can be reversible, but it will require strict adherence to a healthy diet. Do not attempt to treat this on your own. Birds with compromised livers are often fragile, and sudden changes to the diet might actually exacerbate the situation. Always work with a qualified avian veterinarian to decide a course of treatment.

Sometimes, obese parakeets are suffering from hypothyroidism, which slows their metabolism. The thyroid is a small butterfly-shaped gland in the neck, and it relies on iodine to produce needed hormones. Typical seed diets are notoriously low in iodine, and thyroid problems in birds on a seed-only diet are common. An iodine supplement usually helps, but in cases where the thyroid is severely damaged or sluggish, your veterinarian might prescribe synthetic hormones. In budgies, the first sign of trouble is often a goiter, which is a swelling of the thyroid that can press on the trachea and syrinx, making it difficult for the bird to breathe and eat normally. Birds with a goiter will often produce a characteristic high-pitched squeak when they breathe, due to the pressure on their windpipe. Some will vomit if the swelling is pressing on the crop. Again, goiters are reversible, but a veterinarian must rule out other problems, such as tumors or thyroid cancer.

Another common illness that stems from poor nutrition is hypovitaminosis A, which is a fancy term for a vitamin A deficiency. Vitamin A is critical for growth and repair of cell membranes and resistance to infections. Parakeets that don't get enough of this crucial vitamin might display increased thirst, watery droppings, and a runny nose or watery eyes. Frequent sinus infections and digestive tract infections are also common. In severe cases, gout and permanent kidney disease can occur. Again, this is largely caused by a seed-only diet, which supplies very little vitamin A. Feed your parakeet a diet rich in fresh foods such as carrots, broccoli, and dark leafy greens to prevent this deficiency.

Although iodine and vitamin A deficiencies are two of the most common in parakeets, there are dozens of other vitamins, minerals, and trace elements that contribute to good health. Most of these can cause illness or even death if they are missing from your pet's diet. All of the avian veterinarians I've spoken with agree that sub-par nutrition is often either a direct or underlying cause of most companion bird diseases. And, of course, it is the one factor you can control completely.

Bacterial Infections

As mentioned earlier, most bacterial infections are opportunistic and occur secondary to other health problems. Bacteria are everywhere in our environment and in our bodies (and in our keets' bodies as well). In fact, we depend on some bacteria to keep us alive. Various forms of "good" bacteria populate our digestive tracts and help process nutrients, keep dangerous bacteria at bay, and synthesize certain vitamins. It's when the dangerous bacteria gain a foothold due to nutritional lapses or a weakened immune system that infections occur.

Bacterial infections can be localized, such as in the case of an infected wound, or systemic, when the illness spreads through the body. The symptoms will vary accordingly, but digestive and respiratory infections are most common in parakeets. Respiratory symptoms look a lot like a human "cold," and the keet might sneeze, have a runny nose or eyes, or breathe loudly. Birds with sinus trouble might rub their faces along the perch or scratch at their face. Sometimes healthy birds do this to clean their beaks, but a sick bird usually does it more frequently, and the feathers above their nares (nostrils) might look wet or matted. In extreme cases, the budgie might have severe trouble breathing and will grow weak at the slightest exertion.

Digestive upsets are usually characterized by changes in the texture, frequency, or color of droppings. A normal parakeet dropping is comprised of three parts:

solid dark green or brown tubular feces, a bit of white or cream-colored urates, and some clear urine. The color and consistency may change temporarily due to what the bird has recently eaten. For example, beets and berries can stain the droppings red, and lots of watery fruits and vegetables might create more urine. Don't confuse this with diarrhea, in which the feces are runny and typically smelly. True diarrhea is a dangerous sign; wet droppings from healthy fresh fruits and vegetables are not at all a concern. Because of this confusion, some old wives tales persist that say leafy greens are bad for parakeets because they cause diarrhea. This is absolutely not true. Of course, always wash fruits and vegetables thoroughly to reduce any bacteria that might be hitching a ride on the fresh produce. If, however, your bird has runny, smelly, or discolored droppings that don't seem to correlate with a recent meal, or if it is showing any other signs of illness, contact your veterinarian immediately.

Chlamydiosis

Chlamydiosis (also known as psittacosis, ornithosis, or "parrot fever") is a dangerous infection caused by a bacterium known as *Chlamydophila psittaci* (formerly *Chlamydia psittaci*). It is a zoonotic disease, which means that a sick budgie could transmit it to humans. Otherwise-healthy humans usually experience mild to moderate flu-like symptoms that respond quickly to appropriate antibiotics, but it can be life-threatening for elderly or immune-compromised individuals. Although the disease was extremely common back in the days when wild parrots were imported en masse and transported through crowded quarantine stations, better testing and treatment have come a long way in reducing the frequency of infection, especially in today's captive-reared birds.

Chlamydiosis can affect pet birds in many different ways, so it is hard to list "typical" symptoms. In general, budgerigars tend to be sub-clinical carriers, which means that they don't show any obvious symptoms but can transfer the disease to susceptible birds or humans. When they do show symptoms, it's most often respiratory problems and extreme lethargy. There are tests for the disease, and it is treatable. Your veterinarian can advise if he or she feels that testing is necessary.

Avian Polyomavirus (APV)

APV is sometimes also referred to as Budgerigar Fledgling Disease (BFD), which is a misnomer since it can infect any species of parrot. The disease was first described in the 1800s and was called "French Moult" due to its prevalence in Europe at the end of the nineteenth century. It was known to cause high mortality and feather deformities in flocks of breeding budgerigars. Seemingly healthy chicks would die suddenly, and those that survived were known as "runners" because the absence of normal flight and tail feathers made flight impossible. Aviculturists blamed the disease on everything from diet to genetics to mites to overbreeding. It wasn't until more than a century later, in 1981, when researchers discovered that the cause was a virus belonging to the Papovaviridae family.

APV is an unusual disease in many ways. For starters, it affects only unweaned chicks. Although adult birds can carry the virus, it is extremely rare for them to show any symptoms. The disease is easily transmitted from parents to chicks and can be difficult to eradicate. However, birds that survive the infection can sometimes clear the virus from their system and won't necessarily carry it for life. The disease affects many species of birds but can affect them in different ways. For example, most larger species of parrot chicks will die suddenly when exposed to the virus and won't show the feather disorders common to budgies. Because budgies are such common carriers of the disease, it's important to keep baby parrots of other species away from them until they are fully weaned and the danger of likely infection has passed. There are tests and vaccines available, and your veterinarian can advise you if they are necessary for your pet.

Psittacine Beak and Feather Disease (PBFD)

PBFD is caused by Circovirus. This disease occurs in two forms—a chronic form and an acute form—and both are considered fatal. The chronic type disease is most common in mature birds, especially those that have compromised immune systems. However, with excellent supportive care, adult birds suffering from PBFD can live relatively long and quality lives. The virus attacks the feathers and beak structure, causing deformed and missing feathers and crumbling necrotic beaks. Usually, parrots and parakeets with chronic PBFD die from other opportunistic infections, because the virus damages the immune system and leaves the bird open to a host of other infections.

The acute type of the disease is most common among baby birds and is sometimes confused with APV. Both diseases can cause feather abnormalities, but parakeet chicks infected with PBFD will often die quickly after a brief period of lethargy and diarrhea. Those that survive to fledging will continue to lose feathers after each successive molt, whereas chicks that survive APV can eventually grow normal feathers. It does appear that some birds can become infected and clear the virus from their system, but those showing clinical signs of the disease usually survive only about six months to two years from the onset of symptoms.

Scaly Face

Scaly face and leg is a common disorder of parakeets caused by a microscopic mite, *Cnemidocoptes pilae (C. pilae)*. The tiny parasites are typically found near the bird's eyelids, cere, beak, and sometimes legs, where they burrow into the top layers of skin, leaving behind white crusty scales that itch and flake. In advanced cases, the beak and legs can become deformed from a buildup of the scale. Like many diseases and disorders, scaly face is opportunistic and tends to attack individuals that have suppressed immune systems or poor nutritional history. Although there are several folk cures for the mites, it's safer to get a definitive diagnosis from a veterinarian. If it is *C. pilae,* treatment with the drug Ivermectin usually will get rid of the parasites, but you will need to discard wooden perches and clean and disinfect the cage to prevent re-infestation.

The above is just a short summary of some of the more common diseases that can infect parakeets and is by no means a comprehensive list. When your pet is sick or just not quite right, you should always have it examined by a qualified avian veterinarian. It's nearly impossible to diagnose a disease just from the symptoms, which might be vague, overlapping, or even contradictory. Searching the Internet will offer plenty of cures and solemn testimonials, but many of these are misinformed or just plain wrong. Of course, there is good information out there, but if you don't know exactly what you're dealing with, you will only be putting your parakeet at risk. This is why it's crucial to select an avian veterinarian before your keet shows signs of illness. That way, you can provide your keet with efficient and proper medical care.

PARAKEET FIRST AID

Captive chicks that are raised in a cage or aviary have little understanding of what's safe and what's not, so it's up to you to remove potential dangers in the household before they bring harm to your precious parakeet.

In the wild, fledgling parakeets follow and watch their parents to learn about danger. Not all fears are instinctive, but a loud shriek and sudden beak jab from mom or dad sends a clear message: fly away, *fast!* Without this training, the youngsters wouldn't be likely to survive for long in the merciless Outback.

Unfortunately, captive chicks usually don't have that on-the-job training. They are raised in a cage or aviary with little understanding of what's safe and what's scary. Often, they are removed from their parents' care as soon as they are weaned and placed together in a cage with other adolescents. By nature, parakeets are bold and inquisitive little birds. They love to explore and play, and their curiosity is an endearing trait that will make you laugh out loud. Unfortunately, it is a trait that can also get them into trouble.

Household Hazards

When you bring a pet parakeet into your home, you never expect to intentionally cause it harm. Unfortunately, the average household can indeed be a very dangerous place for an unprotected bird. That's why you will need to anticipate and remove these dangers before they bring harm to your feathered pal.

One of the most obvious dangers is other pets. Cats, dogs, ferrets, and snakes are all predators and can quickly kill an unsuspecting keet. Dogs can sometimes be trained to be gentle with birds, but cats are a little less trustworthy. And snakes or ferrets can *never* be trusted around a parakeet. Always supervise out-of-cage time carefully, and do not allow ferrets or snakes to roam free. Your parakeet's cage will not offer it much protection against an agile ferret or hungry snake. Even other parrots can pose a risk. Larger birds tend to be gentle and forgiving of smaller birds, but that's not always the case. Even in play, a much larger bird could seriously injure the smaller parakeet, perhaps fatally. Loose parakeets are also at risk of being stepped on or sat on, crushed in doors, and trapped behind furniture. Don't leave your pet alone when it's loose, even for a brief moment. Like toddlers, they will always find a way to hurt themselves if you're not watching.

Some things that seem perfectly safe to you might be dangerous to your keet. That half-full glass of cold lemonade might be appealing to the bird, which tries to reach for a sip and falls forward into the glass and drowns. Aquariums, open toilets, mop buckets, and dishwater-filled sinks also pose a drowning hazard. Parakeets cannot swim like ducks and geese, and they have no way of escaping from water they can't easily climb out of. Kitchens are especially dangerous, with hot pots filled with boiling liquids and oils.

The list of potential hazards is long, but use common sense and you'll be likely to avoid at least the obvious ones. Some other dangers include:

✔ Cigarettes, candles, and matches. Each of these items can obviously cause serious burns when lit, but they are also toxic when unlit. Just one cigarette butt contains enough nicotine to kill your parakeet if it is ingested. If you are a smoker, secondhand smoke can kill a bird or cause serious respiratory illness, and the nicotine residue on your fingers can cause contact dermatitis on your keet's feet. Maybe your new pet will give you the impetus to quit; if not, please refrain from smoking around your bird, and scrub your hands thoroughly before handling the parakeet.

✔ Houseplants beautify a room and help clean the air, but some are toxic when ingested. Mistletoe, English ivy, and pothos are examples of poisonous plants; African violets, most ferns, and jade plants are considered safe. Check on the Internet or with your veterinarian for a complete list. Be aware that there is often disagreement on these lists. Some plants are listed as safe on one list, and toxic on another. When in doubt, always err on the safe side and assume it's toxic. If your budgie shows an interest in chewing on the greenery, plant some sunflower seeds, radish seeds, wheat berries, or mung beans in organic potting soil and let him munch on the emerging sprouts. Some grocery stores sell little containers of growing wheatgrass for juicing, which make perfect little parakeet gardens.

✔ Ceiling fans, mirrors, and windows all pose a risk for fully flighted birds. These barriers will appear invisible to a parakeet in flight, with disastrous results. Keep your bird's wings

Put a Lid on It!

I once had a startled bird fly straight into a simmering pot of soup. Luckily, I was right behind him and instantly scooped him out and dumped him into the sink, where I quickly ran tepid water over his body to flush away the hot liquid. He survived with just minor burns on his feet—his feathers protected his body from the brief immersion—but I suffered painful burns on both of my hands from diving into the soup pot after him. I shudder to think what would have happened if I had momentarily left the room. My husband still jokes about the time I tried to make parrot stew, but neither the bird nor I thought it was very funny.

safely trimmed, and turn off fans even in the presence of a clipped bird. If your pet is allowed free flight time, cover mirrors and pull shades or drapes over windows.

✔ Household chemicals. This is a widely ranging category that can cover anything from cleaning products to art supplies to personal care items. Almost any substance that is not intended to be edible can be poisonous to a curious parakeet. Your bird doesn't even need to sample the item—skin contact or breathing the fumes can be fatal. Don't let your pet near anything that you wouldn't allow a baby to play with or put in its mouth.

✔ Electrical cords and beaks don't get along. Never allow your bird to chew on cords or play near electrical outlets.

✔ Stained glass fixtures, curtain weights, old paint, and fishing sinkers are just a few of the many household items that probably contain lead. Lead poisoning is often fatal and sometimes hard to detect. Again, do not let your parakeet chew on anything except bird-safe toys and treats.

First Aid

If, despite your best efforts, your parakeet is somehow injured, you will need to get it to a qualified veterinarian as quickly as possible. Sometimes, however, the injury can't wait, and you will need to provide emergency first aid before you can even transport the bird. Or, it might be a minor injury that you can treat at home with your veterinarian's approval. In any case, if you familiarize yourself with the proper procedures in advance, you will be able to react quickly and properly, and perhaps save your pet's life.

Building a Birdie Survival Kit

Keep the following supplies on hand in a water-tight box inside a suitable travel carrier, and add some bottled water and a sealed bag of your parakeet's food. The supplies will cover most first aid needs, and the carrier and food will allow you to quickly grab your pet during an emergency evacuation. Make sure your name and contact information are inscribed or attached to the carrier. It's also a good idea to attach the name and phone number of your veterinarian.

Here's a basic list of what you should include in your kit:
- Gauze squares
- Cotton balls and cotton-tipped swabs
- Stretchy self-adhesive bandaging tape such as Vetrap
- Needle-nosed pliers, locking forceps, or hemostats to pull blood feathers
- Blunt-edged scissors for clipping wings or cutting bandages
- Nail clippers (small dog or cat nail clippers work well for birds)
- Small flashlight with batteries
- Magnifying glass
- Towel for restraint
- Heating pad
- Eyedropper or syringes (without needle) for administering medication or fluids
- Pedialyte or other oral rehydrating agent
- Sterile saline solution
- Hydrogen peroxide 3% solution
- Betadine or other povidone iodine solution
- Thermazene or other water-based antibiotic ointment
- Hand sanitizer (use before handling an injured or ill bird)
- Styptic powder
- Aloe vera gel for mild burns or skin irritations

One of the most common emergencies is bleeding. A healthy 1.4 ounce (40 gram) parakeet has only about 4 milliliters of blood in its body—just slightly over one tenth of an ounce! The loss of more than twenty drops could be fatal. If you see any signs of bleeding, first figure out where the blood is coming from. Minor bleeding from a chipped beak or broken blood feather might resolve on its own without intervention. If it's just a few very tiny drops of blood, calm the bird and observe for a few minutes to see if it stops on its own. Remember that a stressed or struggling bird will bleed faster due to its higher heart rate. If it doesn't stop, a dab of styptic powder or cornstarch can help coagulate bleeding from beaks or toenails, but don't use these on skin wounds. As mentioned in the chapter on Understanding Your Parakeet, broken blood feathers that don't stop bleeding need to be pulled. Use a pair of needle-nosed pliers or locking forceps, and pull the broken feather in the direction of growth.

For larger wounds, rinse the area with hydrogen peroxide or sterile saline solution, and hold gentle pressure with a gauze pad or cotton ball until you can transport your keet to the veterinarian for further treatment. Do not ever try treating a significant blood loss at home. Your bird will most likely need replacement fluids and possibly even a transfusion if it is to survive. Yes, parakeets can receive transfusions using blood drawn from a healthy bird donor, but the procedure is very tricky due to their tiny size and correspondingly low blood volume.

Burns are another household emergency. For small and minor burns, rinse the area carefully in cool (not cold) water, and apply a water-based topical antibiotic burn cream if recommended by your veterinarian. Do not use oil-based formulas, as these will permanently damage feathers. If the burned area is large, or if there's any sign of blistering or severe damage, get the parakeet to a veterinarian for further treatment, including fluid and antibiotic therapy as needed.

Parakeets are playful and acrobatic, but sometimes their shenanigans can result in broken wings or legs. Never attempt to splint a broken bone on your own. In the case of a broken leg, you can temporarily immobilize the limb by cutting a slit in a piece of a plastic straw, and slipping it very gently over the injured leg. If the leg is bent or twisted, however, do not attempt to straighten it; instead, place the bird between some soft rolled towels so that it does not have to place weight on the leg, and take it straight to a veterinarian for proper treatment.

If your parakeet's wing is drooping and appears to be broken, you can very gently immobilize the wing against the bird's body by wrapping a strip of Vetrap or gauze around the body. Be extremely cautious to keep the wrapping loose enough so that it can breathe; avoid crossing over the chest at all, and instead loop the wrap loosely around the upper and lower abdomen, just enough to hold the damaged wing in place. Don't forget that birds need to be able to move their chests to breathe, and

restricting this movement will suffocate them. And remember, this is just a temporary measure until you get to the veterinarian's office. Without appropriate treatment, the bones are unlikely to heal properly, and your parakeet will be permanently disabled even if it does live.

One of the possible life-threatening side effects of any traumatic injury is shock. If the parakeet seems dazed or disoriented, its feathers are fluffed, and it is breathing rapidly, it might be in shock. Place the bird into a heated

carrier in a darkened room and call your veterinarian. If the shock is due to trauma, such as flying into a wall or being attacked by another animal, your pet will need further treatment, possibly radiographs, steroid therapy, or antibiotics. For example, parakeets can suffer from concussions just like humans and might appear uninjured while serious bleeding is occurring in its brain. Never ignore a serious trauma just because the bird is conscious and not obviously damaged. By the time the injury becomes obvious, it might be too late.

Although supplemental heat is almost always a good idea for a sick or injured parakeet, your pet is not impervious to high temperatures. Birds, like people, can suffer from heat exhaustion or heat stroke. Use common sense, and never leave your parakeet unattended in a locked car, even if the windows are rolled down. Symptoms of heat exhaustion include panting, trembling, holding its wings away from its body, or loss of coordination. You must immediately reduce the dangerously high body temperature, or the bird can die. Stand the keet gently in a shallow dish of cool (not cold) water and call your veterinarian. Birds dissipate heat through their feet and legs, so the cool water might help. Do not leave it unattended, however, because it could have a seizure or lose its balance and drown, even in a shallow dish.

While broken bones and bleeding are obvious injuries, there are some dangers that are more insidious to your pet's safety. As mentioned earlier, birds have extremely sensitive respiratory systems, and fumes can be poisonous. That's why old time miners routinely brought canaries into coal mines as early warning detectors for potentially dangerous gas buildups. It's easy to tell from the strong smells of some chemicals that they might be dangerous, but there's a common item in many homes that can emit an odorless and colorless poison that is absolutely deadly to all birds: your non-stick frying pan. Actually, the culprit is the chemical Polytetrafluoroethylene (PTFE), commonly known by the brand name of Teflon. When overheated, Teflon gives off fluorocarbon gases that cause immediate and severe edematous pneumonia in all birds. In essence, blood vessels leak and swell in their lungs, which causes the lungs to fill with fluid.

Affected birds will die rapidly, sometimes gasping in severe respiratory distress before dropping from the perch. Those that don't die immediately can sometimes be saved if they are immediately evacuated to fresh air and treated with antibiotics and diuretics, but the survival rate is not great. The fumes can also sicken humans with mild flu-like symptoms, but people rarely realize that it is cookware that is causing their distress. I recommend ridding your home of all products containing PTFE if you own birds, but it's not as simple as it sounds. Teflon is somewhat ubiquitous, and might be present on items such as irons, ironing board covers, stove burner bibs, and heat lamps. You will need to read labels carefully. Some manufacturers place warning labels on Teflon-coated products, but lack of a warning label doesn't mean the product is safe.

After reading this chapter, you might be surprised to discover all the many ways that a parakeet can get sick or hurt, but don't be discouraged. They are hardy little birds, and most of the bad stuff that can happen never does occur. And if something does go wrong, you'll now be prepared to deal with any emergency in a calm and appropriate manner.

What To Do If Your Parakeet Gets Lost

If you keep your bird's wings carefully trimmed, keep it securely caged on forays out of the house, and keep doors and windows closed when it's out of its cage, this section will never apply to you. Unfortunately, flight feathers grow back quickly, and a startled parakeet only needs a split second to find a loose screen or a door that is slightly ajar in order to escape. That's why it's smart to do a little preparation in advance, just in case you're one of the unlucky owners whose pets take to the sky.

As insurance against the unthinkable, consider these ideas:

✔ Take several full-body color photos of your keet from different angles, and store the images in a safe place. These images can be used to create a "lost bird" poster, or identify your pet if it is found.

✔ Write down any identifying factors, such as missing toes or feather oddities. Of course, if your bird is wearing a band around its leg from the breeder, make sure you write down the band number. Sometimes, even if the bird is safely captured, it's difficult to get it returned if you can't prove ownership. This is more of an issue with larger and more expensive parrots, but it can happen with any pet.

✔ Discuss the advisability of micro-chipping the parakeet with your veterinarian. These tiny capsules are implanted into the breast muscle of birds, and emit a unique code when read with a hand-held scanner. Microchips are quite commonly used to identify larger parrots (and dogs and cats) but some veterinarians are uncomfortable micro-chipping a bird as small as a budgie. The capsule is only about the size of a grain of rice, but that is still a huge implant for such a small bird. It is, however, an absolutely foolproof way to prove ownership, and can help get your pet returned to you if it is found. Most animal shelters routinely scan found animals for the presence of chips, and the companies that sell the devices keep a registry that links the code back to the pets' owners.

The key to retrieving a lost bird is to act quickly. Even in temperate climates, domestically raised pet birds have little chance of survival in the wild. They don't have the skills to search for food, and haven't had any on-the-job training from a parent or flock mate about avoiding predators. They're often bullied or attacked by wild birds, or at the very least exposed to diseases that they have no immunity against. Tame escaped parrots sometimes spontaneously approach a friendly-looking human when they get too cold, hungry, and frightened, but that's no guarantee the human will help or make any attempt to return a tame pet to its owner.

Where To Begin

If your parakeet escapes in front of your eyes, try to stay with the bird. It will likely fly to a nearby tree to get its bearings. Talk softly and calmly, and try to coax it down. If you have trained for the "target" command discussed in Chapter Six, it might come to target if it is not too frightened. Above all, try your best not to show anxiety or fear. Parakeets are masters at discerning human emotion, but sometimes a little dense about pinpointing the cause. It will not understand that you are frightened because it is loose—it will just know that something scary is going on, and it might

try to flee the vague danger. If you have a friend or family member with you, send them back home for the keet's cage and some special treats. Place the cage nearby, and make a happy show of displaying the treat. Pretend to eat some yourself, or offer it to your companion. Eventually, hunger, curiosity, or boredom might win out and your pet will fly down to you. Be very careful about attempting to climb a tree to retrieve a bird; you risk injury, and if the keet is nervous it will likely fly away as soon as you approach.

If you don't know where the bird flew, or you lose sight of it, try walking through the neighborhood while happily calling its name. A tame parakeet is likely to chirp back at you in response, and you might be able to spot it. Also, listen closely for unusual sounds or activity among the native birds. Sparrows especially raise quite a ruckus when an interloper invades their turf. Unfortunately, keets can fly quickly, and it might be out of range before you know it. That's when the time comes to start a "lost bird" campaign.

When you return home, immediately report the escapee to local police, animal hospitals, pet shops, and humane shelters. Don't be discouraged if they act disinterested. Ask them to take down your name and telephone number, and call if they get a sighting. Even gruff police officers can melt at the sight of a helpless and shivering lost pet! Make up as many "lost bird" posters as you can, preferably in color. If you are willing to pay a reward, say so on the poster. Post these in pet shops, grocery stores, libraries, and near playgrounds. Children are often quite good at seeing what adults miss. In fact, if you can, recruit the neighborhood kids to arrange a "search party." (Always get parental approval first, of course). And, if you are aware of any local bird clubs, definitely notify them. Sometimes police and utility workers contact bird clubs when they spot a stray domestic bird.

Until your pet returns home, leave its cage and treats in your back yard, on a deck, or somewhere sheltered near your house. The keet might find its way back, and is likely to be drawn to the safety of its familiar cage. Above all, don't give up. I have heard of many cases where people are reunited with their lost bird after several days or even weeks.

INFORMATION

Magazines and Periodicals

Bird Talk/Birds USA
P.O. Box 6050
Mission Viejo, CA 92690
(949) 855-8822
www.birdchannel.com

The AFA Watchbird
American Federation of Aviculture, Inc.
P.O. Box 91717
Austin, TX 78709-1717
(512) 585-9800
www.afabirds.org/watchbird.shtml

Organizations

Association of Avian Veterinarians
P.O. Box 811720
Boca Raton, FL 33481
(561) 393-8901
www.aav.org

American Federation of Aviculture
P.O. Box 91717
Austin, TX 78709-1717
(512) 585-9800
www.afabirds.org

Budgerigar Association of America
www.budgerigarassociation.org/

Helpful Web Sites

www.upatsix.com
www.budgieplace.com
www.parakeetcare.org

Manufacturers and Suppliers

Cage Catchers
Division of Handy Wacks Corp.
100 E Averill Street
Sparta, MI 49345
(800) 445-4434
www.cage-catchers.com
(custom-made cage bottom liners)

Pretty Bird International, Inc.
31008 Foxhill Avenue
Stacy, MN 55079-9511
(800) 356-5020
www.prettybird.com
(seed, formulated diets, and treats)

Kaytee Products, Inc.
521 Clay Street
Chilton, WI 53014
(800) 669-9580
www.kaytee.com
(seed, formulated diets, and treats)

L'Avian Plus
Highway 75 S
P.O. Box 359
Stephen, MN 56757
(800) 543-3308
www.lavianplus.com
(L'Avian Plus bird diets)

Prevue Pet Products, Inc.
224 North Maplewood Avenue
Chicago, IL 60612
(800) 243-3624
www.prevuepet.com
(pet and breeding cages)

Rolf C. Hagen U.S.A. Corp
305 Forbes Boulevard
Mansfield, MA 02048
(800) 724-2436
www.hagen.com/usa/
(various bird products, cages, seed diets)

Roudybush
340 Hanson Way
Woodland, CA 95776
(800) 326-1726
www.roudybush.com
(pelleted diets)

Age span, 8, 12
Air quality, 29–30
Allergies, 8, 29
Avian polyomavirus, 76, 80–81
Avian veterinarian, 11, 15, 20, 74–76

Bacterial infection, 79
Bathing and grooming, 49–53
Beak, 65, 68–71, 77, 78–79
Bedtime, birdie, 55
Bird out of its cage, 14, 29, 48, 52, 70, 83
Biting, 10, 65
Bleeding, 50–51, 53, 86, 88
Body language, 70–71
Bonding and imprinting, 62–63
Breeder, 13–18, 20, 23, 90
Burns, 84, 86–87

Cage, 8, 15, 25–31, 39, 41, 49
Cage cleaning, 11, 39, 48–49
Cats, 28–29, 33, 62, 75, 83
Children, 8, 10, 18, 33, 38, 47
Chlamydiosis, 76, 79–80
Chores, bird, 25, 47, 49
Colors and mutations, 16–17, 60
Commitment, 9, 23
Companionship, 8–9, 14, 23, 60–62

Daily tasks, 47–48
Diet, 35–45
Digestive upsets, 78
Discomfort signs, 22
Diseases, common, 77–78
Droppings, 48, 71, 77–79
Dry food storage, 39

Elderly people, 10–11
Exercise, 26–27, 56, 68
Eyes, 22–23, 60, 70, 75, 78–79

Fatty tumors, 35, 78
Feathers, 22
Feeder, 27, 29, 62
Female birds, 13–15, 40, 71, 75
First aid, 85–89
Flock mentality, 60–61
Food dishes, 14, 16, 39, 48, 74
Foods to avoid, 42
Fresh foods, 40–41
Fruits, 18, 37, 40–44, 48, 79

Games, 56–57
Grooming, 7, 23, 49–51, 71, 75

Home care, 77
Household hazards, 83–85
Houseplants, 84–85

Illness, signs of, 73–75
Intelligence, 9, 13

Kidney disease, 35, 78

Lead poisoning, 85
Lighting, 30–32
Liver disease, 35, 78
Lost parakeet, 90–91

Maintenance, 7, 11
Male birds, 13–15, 71
Malnutrition, 35, 78–79
Mating, 15
Melanism, 17
Micro-chip, 90
Multiple birds, 14

Obesity, 78

Parakeet
choosing a, 22–23
deciding on, 8–9
pre-owned, 18–19

Parasites, 22–23, 29, 49, 56, 77, 81
Perches, 27–28, 47, 49, 81
Personality, 8
Pet shop, 5, 15, 17–18, 20, 23, 91
Playtime, 53–55
Preening, 23, 57, 61, 66

Quarantine, 33

Respiratory infections, 30, 79
Respiratory symptoms, 78

Safety tips, outdoor, 29
Scaly face and leg, 81
Seeds, 36–40, 42, 44–45, 48
Speech training, 66–67
Squeak, high-pitched, 39, 78
Supplements, 44–45
Survival kit, 86

Taming and training, 65–66
Temperature, 32–33
Toys, 14–15, 18, 47, 49, 53–54, 56–57
Treats, 43–44, 48, 54, 57, 65, 68–69
Trick training, 68–69

Vegetables, 36–37, 41–43, 48, 60, 79
Voice, 9, 55, 65–66

Water dish, 16, 18, 26, 44, 47, 49
Whistling, 11
Wild budgies, 7–8
Wings, 59, 62, 70–71, 74–76, 86–87
Wing trims (clips), 50–52

About the Author

Gayle Soucek has been keeping and breeding a variety of exotic birds for over twenty years. She is the author of seven books and numerous magazine articles on avian husbandry, nutrition, breeding, and disease, and is a contributing writer for *www.webvet.com*. Gayle is past President of the Midwest Avian Research Expo, the Midwest Congress of Bird Clubs, and the Northern Illinois Parrot Society. She resides near Chicago with her husband, birds, dogs, reptiles, and one very laid-back cat.

Acknowledgments

The author would like to thank the veterinarians, researchers, and serious aviculturists who so generously share their time, money, and expertise to help further our understanding of companion bird care.

Important Note

Please remember that parakeets are intelligent and long-lived birds. They require a substantial amount of attention and are not low-maintenance pets. They should never be purchased on a whim. If you are ever unable to care for your parakeet, please contact a local bird shelter for guidance. Releasing a non-indigenous bird into the wild is against the law in most states, and it is a death sentence for the helpless bird.

Cover Credits

Shutterstock: front cover, back cover, inside front cover, inside back cover.

Photo Credits

Dreamstime.com: pages 46, 54, 57, 58, 64, 72; iStockphoto.com: pages 6, 10, 22, 28, 33, 55, 61, 62, 65, 69, 71, 73, 74, 91; Pete Rimsa: pages 50 (bottom), 51 (top and bottom), 52; Shutterstock: pages 2, 4, 5, 7, 9, 12, 13, 14, 15, 16, 17, 18, 19, 21, 23, 24, 25, 27, 30, 31, 32, 34, 35, 36, 37, 38, 41, 42, 44, 45, 47, 48, 50 (top), 53, 59, 60, 63, 66, 67, 76, 79, 80, 82, 83, 84, 87, 88, 92, 93.

All inquiries should be addressed to:
Barron's Educational Series, Inc.
250 Wireless Boulevard
Hauppauge, NY 11788
www.barronseduc.com

Library of Congress Catalog Card No. 2011046399

ISBN-13: 978-1-4380-0026-8

Library of Congress Cataloging-in-Publication Data
Soucek, Gayle.
    Parakeets / by Gayle Soucek.
        p. cm.
    Includes bibliographical references and index.
    ISBN 978-1-4380-0026-8 (pbk.)
    1. Parrots. I. Title.
    SF473.P3S655 2012
    598.7'1—dc23
                                2011046399

Printed in China
9 8 7 6 5 4 3 2 1

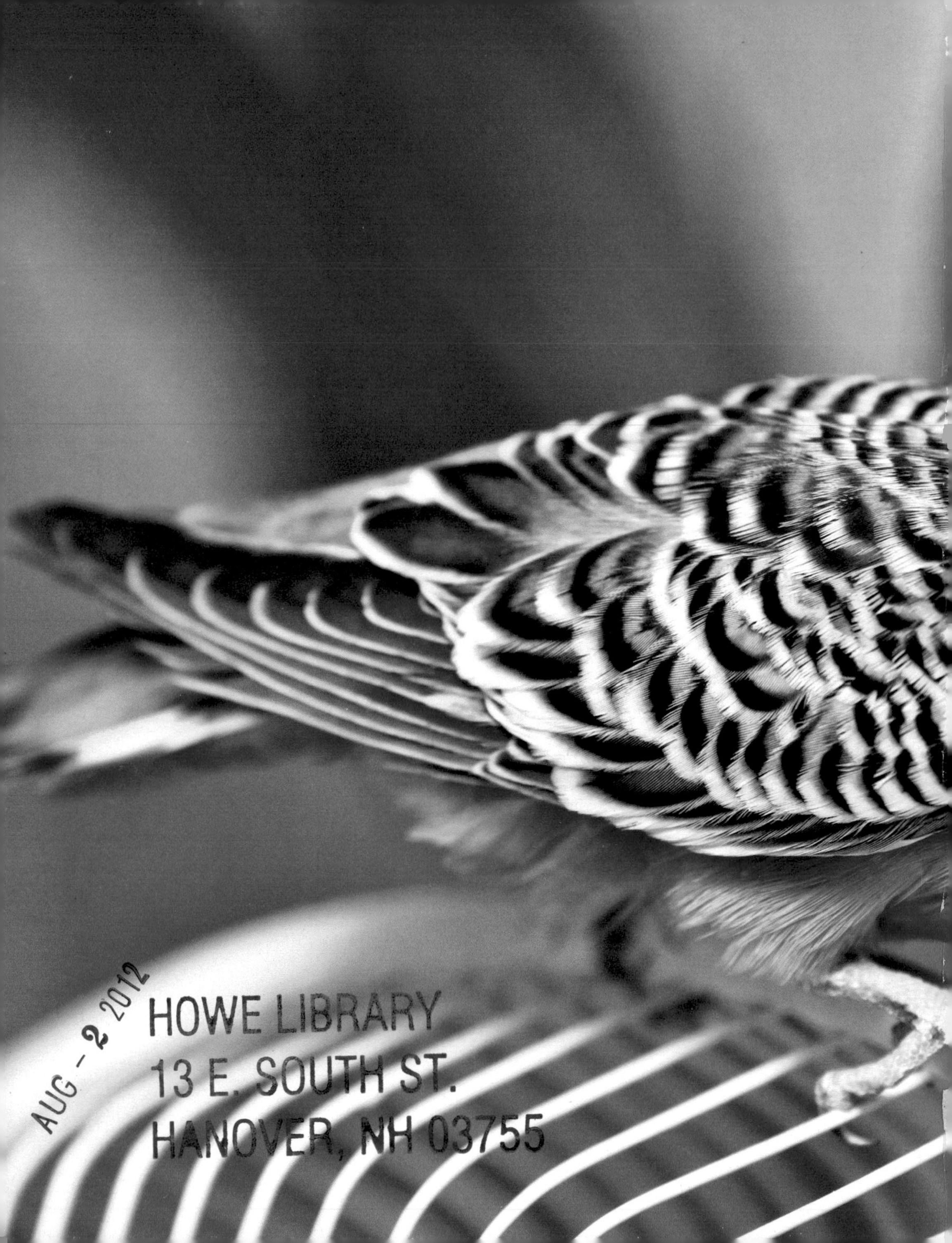